Two Sacred Worlds

Larry D. Shinn

*Experience and
Structure in the
World's Religions*

ABINGDON

Nashville

TWO SACRED WORLDS

Copyright © 1977 by Abingdon

Library of Congress Cataloging in Publication Data

Shinn, Larry D   1942-
   Two sacred worlds.

   1. Religion. 2. Religions. I. Title.
BL48.S516   200   76-45645

ISBN 0-687-42781-9

MANUFACTURED BY THE PARTHENON PRESS AT NASHVILLE, TENNESSEE, UNITED STATES OF AMERICA

Acknowledgments

Countless persons and influences have combined to shape my thoughts as expressed in the pages that follow; yet space would not permit a statement of gratitude sufficient for so many. No influence has been more persistent or real, however, than that represented by the inquisitive musings and challenging assertions of the students it has been my privilege to teach at Oberlin College. It was in answering their puzzlement, and my own, that I initially explored alternate ways to understand what "religion" can mean as a cross-cultural conceptual category if it is to include both the world-detached strivings of Buddhist monks and the passionate, world-affirming devotion to Allah as its expressions. To a great extent this book is a heuristic answer for their many questions. Nonetheless, to three colleagues I owe special gratitude for their thoughtful criticisms, sage advice, and constant encouragement during the actual writing of the manuscript. Harry Thomas Frank, of Oberlin College; Roy C. Amore, of the University of Windsor; and Charles H. Lippy, of Clemson University, all took valuable time from their work to assist me in mine. To each of them I would express deep-felt appreciation. Furthermore, I should be remiss not to thank my typist, Alec Cheloff, who endured my scribbled corrections and his own academic schedule as he typed into the wee hours of many mornings. Finally, my wife and children have not simply borne the burden placed upon a household by such a project but have made the whole experience a joyful one by their patient love. Moreover, my wife, Nancy, still remains a willing helpmate and friendly critic even under the pressure of her own productive career.

For
Nancy,
Christy,
and Robyn

Contents

Introduction

Idries Shah, a contemporary Sufi master, tells the story of an advanced race who lost their superior knowledge and found themselves on a strange island. Only a small cadre of master shipbuilders retained their memory of their previous paradise and the shipbuilding skills necessary to lead the other Islanders back home someday. As the time approached for a safe return to their former paradise, the shipbuilders began slowly to educate young people in the arts of shipbuilding and swimming. As the first ships were being built, some of the Island revolutionaries began debunking such nonsense. Recognizing the heavy demands shipbuilding placed on the commoners, the revolutionaries appealed to the masses to come to their senses and to stop working toward the illusory paradise the shipbuilders talked about. The revolutionaries would taunt, "If there is any reality in ships and swimming, show us ships which have made the journey, and swimmers who have come back!"

The revolutionaries developed their rhetoric into a complete, simplistic system marked by the new mental process called "reason." This new gospel proclaimed that anything that could not be seen or was not approved by the values of society was "irrational" and therefore deluded and evil. This new liberating gospel was accepted by the masses, though imperfectly, as a liberating word. It was easy to accept the claims of this new teaching since there was much evidence on the Island to confirm the claims of "reason" and support the view that it was not healthy to think beyond the life of the Island.

Initially, many of the shipbuilders were hanged for treason and many swimmers were killed. But as the life of the Island grew more complex, even those who were "irrational" were tolerated, though occasionally persecuted. And some shipbuilders survived. Some still talk of a life beyond the Island.[1]

Anyone venturing into the oft traveled yet treacherous waters of religious studies must feel a bit like one of the Islanders who forgot all he ever knew about life beyond the Island. The shipbuilders and the revolutionaries both speak with a confidence often not shared by the doubting but adventuresome Islander who finds claims to "secret knowledge" and "rational knowledge" equally problematic. This book is written as an attempt by an inquisitive Islander to explore and to explicate the relationship between the personal and private religion of the master shipbuilder and the social and institutional forms of religion as analyzed by the "rational" revolutionaries.

It is assumed that only an analysis that takes into account both the personal experience of the devout and the religious life acquired through socialization processes will fathom both the personal *and* social dimensions of the religious life. More important, only such an analysis can explore patterns of relationship and interdependence of religious phenomena (myth, ethics, etc.) personally conceived and expressed in the context of religious institutions and their life that operate within and reflect a particular social and cultural milieu. It is the task of this study to indicate these patterns of relationship and interdependence as they are found in various religious traditions of the world. Consequently, I have chosen three religious traditions—Hebrew religion, early Christianity, and monastic Buddhism—from which examples will systematically be taken to demonstrate the interrelationship of personal and social religion. The first two sets of examples are taken from the two religious traditions basic to American (and Western) cultures, while the Buddhist examples provide a stark contrast in conceptualization and cultural setting and give the theoretical framework broader application among the world's great religious traditions.

Two Sacred Worlds

Students of religion are familiar with the distinction commonly made between *sacred* and *profane* modes of existence. This distinction was observed early in this century by Arnold van Gennep,[2] Emile Durkheim,[3] and others, but was popularized and explicated more fully in the work of Mircea Eliade written in 1956 and entitled *The Sacred and the Profane.* According to Eliade, *"sacred* and *profane* are two modes of being in the world, two existential situations assumed by man in the course of history."[4] The essential difference between these two perceptions of the world is their respective acceptance and rejection of a Sacred Power or Reality which stands over against the everyday, commonsense world of experience.

Following Rudolf Otto's understanding of the "holy" or "sacred," Eliade says, "The sacred is equivalent to a *power,* and, in the last analysis, to *reality.* The sacred is saturated with being." Therefore, a person endowed with a religious perspective lives with a "sense of the sacred," and the Sacred is that powerful and mysterious reality which presents itself as that "something there" beyond everyday events and experiences.[5] The Sacred may be a god such as Allah or a more diffuse power, such as the Chinese Tao or the Hindu's Brahman. On the other hand, a person operating within a profane viewpoint is one who lives, makes value judgments, and determines what is real without reference to a Sacred Reality. Consequently, sacred and profane are not two separate worlds or sets of objects, but are two different human interpretations or experiences of the same empirical world.[6] What may be a simple stone to a person with a profane outlook may be the location of a Sacred Power to be handled with awe and reverence to the person living within a religious realm.

What this study proposes to do is to examine the nature of the sacred mode of existence according to its twofold sources of origination: personal experience and social conditioning. Moving beyond the twofold perspectives of sacred and profane, therefore, the following chapters will elucidate two different dimensions of the religious life itself. By focusing on the inception of religious traditions, while taking cognizance of the social factors in the rise and growth of such traditions, we may come to see that there are really two sacred worlds in which persons can live beyond profane interpretations. As is the case with the realms of the sacred and profane, the two sacred worlds of personal and social religiosity are different spheres of existence, not in an objective but rather in an experiential sense.

The assumption that underlies the assertion that there are essentially two different realms of the sacred is that the sources of the experiences that give rise to the religious life will determine the nature of that life. Therefore, an immediate experience of a Sacred Power (a hierophany) may give rise to a personal religious life quite different from the religiosity of a person who, in a later time, enters that same religious tradition through socialization processes. Therefore, one sacred world, or type

14

of religious life, arises as a product of the emotions and attitudes aroused by an experience of a Sacred Power. This is the sacred world of personal religion. Chapter 1 explores the nature and meaning of religious experience and the impetus it provides toward the formation of this personal realm of religiosity.

The second sacred world originates in the processes of socialization, comprising experiences in the home, the religious institution, and other such influential social groups. The phrase "social religion" will be used to indicate this realm of living. Chapter 2 discusses social religion as a second type of religiosity, which springs from social processes. It is here that the functions and priorities of religious institutions are most important. Myths, rituals, ethical proclamations, and dogmatic assertions may arise in the context of personal religion, though they gain their final character in the social processes of the religious institution's ordering of the religious life. Social or cultural parochiality, as well as the institutional focus, marks social religion as a way of life distinguishable from personal religion.

Although there are many people who live primarily in one or the other of these sacred worlds exclusively, the two worlds of personal and social religion overlap and are, at least initially in a religion's history, sequential and interdependent. For example, myths and rituals may arise as attempts to explicate and to re-create original experiences of the Sacred, but since the very language used to tell of one's encounter with the Sacred is culturally determined and the elements of ritual usually are taken from the secular context, it is a short step from personal explanation and action to an institutionalization of those statements and actions. Chapter 3 will deal with this interdependence of personal and institutional forms of myth and ritual.

Based upon the assumption that a person's behavior is a function of his or her experience, ethics may be thought of in the sacred world of personal religion as "existential imperatives." The ethics of social religion may be refined by reflection and amended or expanded by social needs and interests, but initially it is the impulse gained from experience of the Sacred that directs one to act in certain ways. Chapter 4 will relate this twofold analysis of religious "oughts."

Chapter 5 will focus on the development of reflective myths in the social context of the various religions and suggest their relationship to the expressive myth of religious experience. Filling the personal need to understand one's experiences of the Sacred in the context of the everyday world, reflective myths explain beginnings, explicate the relationship of the Sacred to other areas of life, and defend the Sacred (and one's experience of the Sacred) against disbelievers and critics. Dogma and theology are simply extensions of this same social process.

What follows is admittedly only the bare bones of an analysis of the complex structural relationships and interdependences of religious phenomena. Still, if the student of religion senses the necessity for a closer examination of religious traditions from the dual points of view presented below, then I shall consider my efforts to have been rewarded. What is implied in such an approach is that there are structural connections between religious assertions (theology and dogmas) and activities (ritual and ethical) that must be understood from the perspectives of personal experience and social process. Therefore, I have tried to untangle the major connective threads that tie personal experience to social form and content. Certainly, more data and a greater variety of traditions than I use here must be marshaled to demonstrate the full extent and applicability of this analytical design. However, I not only argue a theoretical model in what follows, but I also apply that approach to three major religious traditions. I leave it to my readers to decide the extent to which I have succeeded in relating and exemplifying the structures of two sacred worlds.

Chapter 1
The Religion of
Personal Experience

Thesis

One sacred world is that which encompasses religion that originates in personal experience. Put differently, a sacred world is a systematic interpretation of life experiences that includes the claim of a Sacred Power, and one such perceptual world may be initiated from experiences understood as personal contact with a Sacred Reality (i.e., from a religious experience). This sacred mode of existence may be called personal religiosity, as its roots are to be found in personal religious experiences. The socializing forces of institutional religion may or may not be directly involved in the formation of personal religiosity, since the catalyst for personal religion, and its life, lies beyond social precedents and norms for the most part. Therefore, personal religious behavior and conceptualization share a common religious experience and are to be distinguished from the behavior and conceptualizations that proceed from socialization processes.

Religious Experience and the Rise of Religion

A contemporary psychologist, R. D. Laing, says, "Certain *transcendental experiences* seem to me to be the original wellspring of all religions."[1] Laing continues, "People did not first 'believe in' God: they experienced His presence, as was true of other spiritual agencies." Therefore, according to Laing, religious faith is not a matter of believing but a matter of experience. He views contemporary criticisms of religion as the result not so much of the triumph of reason as of the failure of experience. What is at stake in such a claim is the very nature of religion, and, thereby, religious studies. Depending upon which assumptions are made about the essential nature of religion, a student of religion will proceed to investigate data and to make conclusions excluding those questions which the chosen axioms deem unimportant or inappropriate. For example, agreeing with Laing's postulate about the primacy of experience, Michael Novak is led to define religion as personal conversion to a sacred world:

> Religion, I want now to propose, is primarily a conversion to the sense of the sacred. By conversion I mean a focusing of one's way of life: I mean taking up one standpoint, after having occupied another. . . . To be religious, then, is to experience a hierophany [manifestation of the sacred]. . . . It is to be centered.[2]

This claim for one sphere of sacred awareness as being personal and experiential is not new. William James, who wrote for another generation, says in *The Varieties of Religious Experience* (1902):

> It would profit us little to study this second-hand religious life [i.e., institutional religion]. We must make search rather for the original experiences which were the pattern-setters to all this mass of suggested feeling and imitated conduct. These experiences we can only find in individuals for whom religion exists not as a dull habit, but as an acute fever rather.[3]

As implied, James makes a distinction between "religion pure and simple" and institutional religion.[4] He analyzes only the personal aspects of religion because, for him, they are more fundamental than either theology or ecclesiastical studies.[5] James assumes that religious experience has a generative function, and therefore his position has been summarized as saying: "religion originates in and always remains essentially something within the experience of the individual."[6]

Following Laing, James, and others, a fundamental assertion of this study, then, is that one mode of religion—personal religion—arises and gains its character from personal experiences of that which is considered a Sacred. Furthermore, it is assumed that religious awareness that arises from personal experiences stands sequentially prior to the organization of religious institutions and therefore must be considered in any analysis of institutional religion. These two postulates are demonstrated in the analysis of several religious traditions that follows. Consequently, this notion of personal religion is not derived from psychological theory but is a descriptive category that can aid the study of various religious traditions. However, psychological categories can provide generally understood terminology to aid later descriptions, and it is to such formulations I would now turn.

Abraham Maslow uses the term "peak experience" to designate ecstatic or transcendent experiences often identified with religion. Peak experiences contain unusually profound emotional or intellectual value for a person. These experiences are not restricted to the realm of religion alone, but may describe any experience that is "deep and meaningful." As such, peak experiences are "the raw materials out of which not only religions can be built but also philosophies of any kind: educational, political, aesthetic."[7]

To recognize that such experiences may or may not be religious necessitates our identifying those characteristics which may serve to differentiate religious from nonreligious peak experiences. Problems of terminology are exemplified by the following two descriptions of peak experiences. One of the experiences was drug-induced; the other was not.

A's experience:

Suddenly I burst into a vast, new indescribably wonderful universe. Although I am writing this over a year later, the thrill of the surprise and amazement, the awesomeness of the revelation, the engulfment in an overwhelming feeling-wave of gratitude and blessed wonderment, are as fresh, and the memory of the experience is as vivid, as if it had happened five minutes ago. And yet to concoct anything by way of description that would even hint at the magnitude, the sense of ultimate reality . . . this seems such an impossible task. The knowledge which has infused and affected every aspect of my life came instantaneously and with such complete force of certainty that it was impossible, then or since, to doubt its validity.

B's experience:

All at once, without warning of any kind, I found myself wrapped in a flame-colored cloud. For an instant I thought of fire . . . the next, I knew that the fire was within myself. Directly afterward there came upon me a sense of exultation, of immense joyousness accompanied or immediately followed by an intellectual illumination impossible to describe. Among other things, I did not merely come to believe, but saw that the universe is not composed of dead matter, but is, on the contrary, a living Presence; I became conscious in myself of eternal life. . . . I saw that all men are immortal: that the cosmic order is such that without any peradventure all things work for the good of each and all; that the foundation principle of the world . . . is what we call love, and that the happiness of each and all is in the long run absolutely certain.[8]

In trying to answer the question, Which experience was drug-induced and which one was not? one recognizes a similarity of peak experiences associated with a Sacred

Power and those which make no such claim. In fact it may be appropriate to ask if the presence or absence of a drug stimulus necessarily serves as a qualifying distinction between nonreligious and religious experiences. Certainly a descriptive analysis of these two experiences could proceed without having knowledge of which was the drug-induced one. Still, my intent is to indicate what may be said to be "religious" about a certain peek experience.

In describing transcendental (i.e., "mystical") experiences, James notes four basic features: (1) ineffability, (2) noetic quality, (3) transiency, (4) passivity.[9] Ineffability is the feeling that a peak experience "defies expression." For example, Person A above says it is an "impossible task" to describe his experience, while Person B concurs, saying his experience contained an "illumination impossible to describe." It is not uncommon to hear statements such as "I can't explain it to you" or "You've got to experience it for yourself" from persons who claim to have had peak experiences. In other words, peak experiences (religious or not) cannot be fully described or recreated verbally. From one point of view, ineffability may be viewed as the inability of language to relay the emotional content of peak experiences. In the context of religious experiences, ineffability may be described as the failure of language to capture the subject of the experience, i.e., the Sacred. Whatever the case, persons who assert that they have insufficient language to express the essential character of their peak experience often utilize analogies, metaphors, and symbolic language to indicate the nature of their experience.[10]

Although peak experiences may defy precise description, they are nevertheless accepted, according to James, as "states of knowledge" (i.e., they are noetic). But the knowledge or illumination received cannot be grasped by

the discursive intellect. Knowledge associated with revelation, illuminations, and other peak experiences often is
described not in the propositions of the logician but in
enigmatic generalizations that, all the same, carry great
authority for the experiencer. Note that Person A refers to
"the knowledge which has infused and affected every
aspect of my life" and which "came . . . with complete
force of certainty." While not stating the content of that
illuminating knowledge precisely, Person A found it
"impossible . . . to doubt its validity." Person B describes
his or her "intellectual illumination" by including as part
of its content a vision of a "living Presence" (opposed to a
"universe of dead matter") and a consciousness of
"eternal life." *It is precisely an awareness of a Sacred
Power as the noetic content of religious experiences that
differentiates those experiences from other dramatic
(peak) experiences.* While an aesthetic or political peak
experience may be characterized by ineffability, transiency, and passivity, only religious experience brings
with it, so it seems, a consciousness of an encounter with
a Sacred Reality.

Transiency and passivity may be considered to be
usual, but not necessarily essential, marks of religious
experiences. Like all peak experiences, the peak religious
experience is usually of short duration. That is, the state of
ecstasy is momentary. Furthermore, a person's memory
must be the bearer of such states until further experiences
of the same kind are repeated. However, active attempts to
repeat peak experiences may be self-defeating, since
passivity—marked by suspension of the will of the
experiencer—is a usual characteristic of peak experiences.
Willful preparations (e.g., stages of meditation) may be
made, but the peak experience itself seems not to be
controlled by the individual. A person who looks at the
sunset every evening does not pick *the one* sunset that is

experienced as an aesthetic peak. Likewise, a Zen novice may try for years to achieve illumination in *Zazen* (meditation) only to have satori (divine illumination) come to him as he works in his garden.

Joachim Wach, a noted historian of religion of more recent decades, utilizes James and Rudolf Otto as he enumerates four criteria he considers absolutely necessary to name an experience "religious."[11] Like James, Wach insists that the experiences that are genuinely religious include an awareness or perception of an Ultimate Reality. Consequently, religious experiences are understood as encounters with an external Power or Reality that involves the whole person in his or her thinking, feeling, and willing capacities (Wach's second criterion). From Wach's perspective, there cannot be a "godless" (I would say "Sacredless") religion, since any claim to an Ultimate Reality that, in fact, is finite is merely pseudo-religious. Marxism is an example of what Wach considers a pseudo religion to be. The third characteristic of religious experience Wach delineates is "intensity." Here Wach is describing not only the experience itself, but also the psychological aftereffects. He says, "Potentially this is the most powerful, comprehensive, shattering, and profound experience of which man is capable." Continuing from this notion of intensity with regard to religious experiences, Wach states, "The fourth criterion of genuine religious experience is that it issues in action. It involves imperative; it is the most powerful source of motivation and action." As will be explained in chapter 4, it is obvious that experiences of a climactic sort do not all result in a new or "reborn" life. On the other hand, it is clearly the case that *all* religious traditions expect behavior to be transformed in initiates who claim experience of the Sacred Power, however that Power is understood or characterized. With his fourth criterion,

Wach rightly recognizes the difference between religion as a world view and religion as a mode of living.

In this study, peak religious experiences will be designated by the category "immediate religious experiences." Consequently, immediate religious experiences will be delimited by the attributes of ineffability and noesis delineated by James *and* the emphasis on intensity culminating in an altered impulse to act in accord with received illumination noted by Wach. I would stress, therefore, the emotional *and* mental content of such experiences as these are expressed in behavior. I would, however, qualify the content of noetic illumination to include as religious only those experiences which recognize a Sacred, a Power from beyond, which has intruded. This qualification provides a distinction between the illumination of the philosopher and that of the religious person. Likewise, such a distinction brings to attention what it is that separates religious experiences from other deep, meaningful ones.

As I said in the Introduction, I follow Rudolf Otto (and those who use him—such as Mircea Eliade and Michael Novak) in understanding the Sacred to be equivalent with a Reality experienced as mysterious and powerful. That is, unlike some common usages that reduce "sacred" to an object or principle of greatest worth (e.g., money or love), my position is that persons who have religious experiences assert an *encounter* with Something or Someone *other* than themselves. Consequently, whether the Sacred is perceived as a god (e.g., Allah) or a non-god (e.g., Tao) it is experienced as an *agent* of action or, at least, of self-revelation. Otto says that The Holy (i.e., Sacred) is experienced as a "mysterious Power." [12] A Sacred Reality must, by definition, be encountered as mysterious because it breaks into finite and human consciousness as a partially understood Otherness, and it is known to be tremendous and powerful by the feelings of awe and "creatureliness" it evokes. As a mysterious and therefore ineffable Power, the Sacred represents more than just that which is held to be valuable or meaningful. Therefore, for this study Sacred will be use to refer to that "wholly other," mysterious Power which is encountered in religious experiences. Following this lead, we can understand an immediate religious experience as involving both emotional and mental stimulation that, to the experiencer, occurs as the result of an encounter with an ineffable and powerful Other.

Given the above context, it should be apparent why immediate religious experiences are often conversion experiences. That is, as dramatic confrontations with a Sacred Power (god or non-god) immediate religious experiences have the capability to redirect a person's life focus and perception. A new standpoint is assumed. Examples of this are to be seen in both Moses' experience of Yahweh and the Buddha's enlightenment. However, there is a second type of religious experience, which is not as dramatic as immediate experience. I choose to call such experiences *cumulative*.[13] Marked by no specific occasion(s) of direct, immediate experience of the Sacred, cumulative religious experience is composed of those events which, when tallied by personal reflection, lead a person to claim an "experience" of the Sacred leading to her or his personal religion. There may be personal experiences (e.g., of nature or of other "holy" persons) that lead an individual to claim such awareness, though not direct experience, of a Sacred Power. Those experiences which lead to a cumulative awareness of the Sacred are marked more by their cognitive than their emotional content. Horace Bushnell's description of Christian nurture exemplifies the cumulative type of religious experience in a Christian context:

There is then some kind of nurture which is of the Lord, deriving a quality and a power from Him, and communicating the same. ... [Therefore,] *the child is to grow up a Christian, and never know himself as being otherwise.* In other words, the aim, effort, and expectation should be ... that he is to open on the world as one that is spiritually renewed, not remembering the time when he went through a technical experience."[14]

To talk about cumulative religious experience necessitates using the word "experience" in a collective sense— i.e., recognizing that not one but many events lead to an awareness of the Sacred. This usage corresponds to such secular statements as "my experience with her leads me to believe she is an honest person." In such a building-block fashion, cumulative events may add up to an awareness of the Sacred that is recognized in a validating confirmation of belief that falls short of a direct experience of the Sacred.

Experiences that lead to personal religion, therefore, may best be described as fitting on an experiential continuum ranging from immediate to cumulative. To posit such a continuum recognizes the variety of religious experiences by virtue of the extent to which they relate the Sacred (immediate experience———cumulative awareness), as well as the extent to which either emotional or cognitive features dominate the experience (ecstatic———subdued). It is important to recognize that personal religion need not arise only from immediate experiences, although they very often are the source. Furthermore, a person may have both kinds of experiences. A mix may occur such that cumulative experiences precede immediate ones. Bushnell's own experience confirms such a sequence: "It came to him at last, not as something reasoned out, but as an inspiration, a revelation from the mind of God himself."[15]

27

It should be obvious that several continuums might profitably be used to describe religious experiences. One such continuum would include the mode of experience— *i.e.*, whether the experience was a *direct* confrontation with the Sacred (as in Zen's *satori* or a Sioux's vision) or an *indirect* encounter through a mediator (as in an incarnation of God such as Jesus or through a Hebrew's experience of historical events). Such a continuum merits attention because the indirect experience, by definition, asserts that the Sacred is not only revealed, but also veiled, by the channel (e.g., sacred book or person) that conveys the experience. It follows, therefore, that direct religious experiences nearly always are immediate, whereas indirect experiences more often give rise to a cumulative sense of the Sacred. The two continuums are, to a great degree, parallel dimensions of an analysis of religious experience.

A third continuum that can be used would describe religious experiences in terms of their balance between emotional and rational qualities. This continuum further elucidates the gulf that can exist between immediate and cumulative experiences of the Sacred. It is the feelings and the reason of humankind that are opposed in such classical dialectics as that of Dionysus and Apollo. Such a continuum indicates the degree of the balance of emotions and reason. Seldom is either quality completely dominant or absent. As I have said earlier, both emotional excitement and noetic illumination are present in immediate religious experience. Both qualities are present in cumulative experiences too. The major distinction between the two types of experience is the tendency for emotional content to be high in immediate experiences and for cognitive factors to be dominant in gradual religious experiences. Ecstatic visions of the plains Indians would be an example of the emotional, immediate religious experience. Bushnell's own experience is an example of the blend of the two.

In summary, this discussion points to several continuums that tend to parallel one another:

Immediate Religious Experience ———
                    Cumulative Religious Experience
Direct Access to the Sacred ———
                    Indirect Access to the Sacred
Emotional Content Dominant ———
                    Rational Content Dominant

This typology of religious experience will be useful in making distinctions between the indirect and cumulative Exodus experience of the Hebrew people and the more direct experience of nirvāṇic bliss by the Buddha.

To those examples let us now turn.

The Hebrew Exodus

Yahwist religion, often called Israelite religion, offers a clear example of the role religious experience plays in inaugurating a new religion. Its incompleteness as an example arises from what scholars do not know about the history of the Mosaic community and the experiences that gave rise to the religious tradition that honors Yahweh as the Sacred Power. Its aptness arises from the rather clear role the Exodus, as a cumulative religious experience, performs in the formation of early Yahwism.

Yahwism arose in a cultural milieu that included religious groups as varied as the priestly state religion of the Egyptians and the clan religions of nomadic Arabian tribes. It has been suggested that the patriarchal religions centering around the God of Abraham (Gen. 12:7 and 24:12), the God of Isaac (Gen. 26:24-25), and the God of Jacob (Gen. 28:12-16) were examples of clan religion.[16]

Regardless of such a claim, it is certain that clan religion was an influential phenomenon in the Middle East at the time of Moses.[17] Two basic features of clan religion were: (1) the connection of the clan deity to the head person of the clan, and (2) the reference to such a deity as "god of your father."[18] This type of religious expression was common in the Old Akkadian (twenty-fifth through twenty-third centuries B.C.) and Old Assyrian (twentieth through ninetieth centuries B.C.) periods, when frequently divinities were named as the "father of ..." or "kinsman of ..." a particular individual. The Moses tribes were, after their departure from Egypt, a seminomadic, shepherding people who might be expected to reflect the clan religions of other Israelite or nomadic tribes. This was not to be the case, for while Yahweh shares some features common to clan deities (associated with mountains, acts in close relationship to "his" people), the religion begun by the seminomadic Hebrews in the Arabian desert and completed by the settlers of Canaan broke the mold of its antecedents and its contemporaries.[19] The story of the Exodus is the place to begin to understand the Hebrews' religiosity.

The Exodus from Egypt of Moses and the tribes that followed him is only one of several Semitic migrations. (Georg Fohrer refers to four "waves of Semitic migration," which span two thousand years from c. 3000 B.C. to 900 B.C.)[20] It is clear, however, that the Moses-led journey was, for Hebrew religion, the most significant. The book of Exodus relates the sacred story of the flight from Egypt by the Moses host from the birth of Moses, his early life, his sojourn in Midian, his call by Yahweh, and subsequent events leading to his death. The sacred history of the Hebrews is succinctly summarized in a later creedal formulation:

A wondering Aramean was my father; and he went down into Egypt and sojourned there, few in number; and there he became a nation, great, mighty, and populous. And the Egyptians treated us harshly, and afflicted us, and laid upon us hard bondage. Then we cried to the Lord the God of our fathers, and the Lord heard our voice, and saw our affliction, our toil, and our oppression; and the Lord brought us out of Egypt with a mighty hand and an outstretched arm, with great terror, with signs and wonders; and he brought us into this place and gave us this land, a land flowing with milk and honey. (Deut. 26:5-9; see also Josh. 24:2-14)

The historical accuracy of different elements of the account given in Exodus has been a matter of debate. There are, however, certain events related to the Exodus of Moses' tribes that appear to have been established through historical and archaeological investigation. Fohrer lists six of these conclusions: (1) the Moses tribes in Egypt were distinct from other Israelite tribes already settled in Palestine; (2) the journey of Moses to Midian and his relationship to Jethro, a priest of the Midianite god, Yahweh, did occur; (3) the departure and escape from Egypt of Moses' tribes happened during Egypt's struggle with several foreign foes (approximately 1234–1230 B.C.); (4) there was a prolonged stay at the oasis of Kadesh, where Moses and his people were joined by the Levites, who also worshiped Yahweh; and (5) a journey to a sacred mountain (called Sinai by J, Horeb by D, and "Mountain of God" by E) took place where the relationship between Yahweh and his people was strengthened; and (6) the journey ended with the settlement of Canaan.[21] In concluding, Fohrer says of the Exodus, "It is associated with the recollection of a miraculous experience: deliverance from the pursuing Egyptians at Lake Sirbonis on the Mediterranean coast."

An account of Moses' own experience of Yahweh is related in the story of his encounter with a burning bush

31

(Exod. 3:1 ff). Yet even if this story were completely accurate, such an immediate experience of the Sacred by Moses in Midian could hardly be transferred to his fellow Hebrews back in Egypt. What can be said of Moses' experiences (burning bush, Sinai encounter, etc.) is that they were, if they occurred as reported, immediate and direct. Contrariwise, the basic religious experience of the Moses host as a whole was a series of events that were experienced as repeated interventions of Yahweh and were interpreted cumulatively as the "Exodus event." This would suggest that the personal experience of Yahweh by Moses was not transferable to his people and that only a gradual awareness of Yahweh in the Exodus events provided for the Hebrews an experience all their own. It was not one event, then, but many which made up the Exodus experience for the Hebrew people.

Clearly, Moses' part in the Exodus drama was not coincidental. While he could not transfer to others his own experience of Yahweh, it was a guiding interpretive force. Fohrer says of Moses and the Exodus event: "He helped bring the events about, interpreted them brilliantly, and sought to keep alive the religious forces awakened by these events, guiding them into proper channels." Therefore, it was the cumulative experience of the wandering Moses host plus the interpretations provided by Moses (i.e., Yahweh as the source of the Exodus liberation) that sparked in the Hebrews a desire to give awe-filled devotion to Yahweh. To the Moses tribes, the same Yahweh Moses had encountered in the desert now had intervened in historical and natural events on their behalf. Whatever the previous nature and history of Yahweh, in the Exodus event he had become the Hebrew's Sacred and they his people.[22]

We have already seen that the Mosaic Yahweh bore resemblances to the Ancient Near Eastern clan divinities.

The Exodus account specifically identifies Yahweh as the same deity known to Abraham, Isaac, and Jacob (Exod. 3:6, 14-16). The intimate relationship between Yahweh and his chosen people Israel is expressed again and again in various contexts with words such as "I will take you for my people, and I will be your God." (Exod. 6:7; compare 20:2). A basic attribute of Yahweh, therefore, is his personal attachment to the people called Israel.

From the perspective of the Hebrew people, theirs was an experience of being protected and encompassed as a chosen people by a powerful deity named Yahweh. In the events of the Exodus, the Hebrews encountered a mighty power acting on their behalf. His very name indicates that Yahweh is a "dynamic and effectual presence" (from the Hebrew rootword "to be").[23] Yahweh was experienced to be angry and loving, jealous and kind, vengeful and forgiving. No other gods were his equal (Exod. 20:2-3). This assertion on behalf of Yahweh set him apart from other clan deities. He was a god above all other gods, more powerful than all other gods. Consequently, if any one characteristic of the Yahweh experienced in the Exodus were to be singled out, it would be his terrible or awesome power. So powerful and mysterious was Yahweh that even the recitation of his name was forbidden. Such was the Sacred Power experienced by the Hebrews in the Exodus event, and to such a cumulative experience I would attribute the genesis of Yahwism. Applying Laing's observation to this specific tradition, we can conclude that the Hebrews did not first believe in Yahweh, they experienced his powerful presence.

The Christian Incarnation

While the Hebrews experienced a Sacred Power in events of history, the early Christians claimed revelation through a historical person, namely, the man Jesus. The

33

earliest Christian community might be considered, from one point of view, a Jewish sect. However, its point of departure from Jewish sectarianism and, indeed, eventually from Judaism itself, was its allegiance to Jesus as the promised Messiah (*Christos* in Greek). Rudolf Bultmann states well the significant breaking point:

> But the history of Israel is no longer their [early Christians'] own history. They ceased, for instance, to regard the Jewish festivals as re-enactments "for us" of the events of the past. When he speaks of the foundation of the Church, Paul no longer points to the exodus from Egypt. The event by which the Church is constituted is the death of Christ.[24]

Therefore, early Christianity broke with its mother tradition in its very foundation experience, yet Jewish and even Hellenistic concepts and expectations shaped the disciples' experience of the man Jesus.[25] On the one hand, Jewish apocalyptic speculation and sectarian messianic expectations clearly influenced the early disciples' perception of Jesus.[26] On the other hand, Hellenistic language (*e.g., Christos*) and concepts (*e.g., logos*) were utilized by the early Christian community to explicate Jesus' life and message.[27] Regardless of whether one places the early Christian understanding of Jesus primarily in a Jewish messianic or in a Hellenistic philosophical and religious context, any claims to a single or a simple-minded adoption of such expectations and speculation seems unwarranted.

What complicates any attempt to describe the historical Jesus is the complexity and nature of the scriptural traditions handed down to us. The main lines of Jesus' life and teachings are told in the four Gospels ("good news") of the New Testament. Matthew, Mark, and Luke are called the Synoptic Gospels, as they commonly share several oral traditions, which they use to present Jesus and his message. The latest Gospel written is John, although elements of its oral traditions may likely antedate much of what is found in the Synoptic Gospels. All four books are sacred biographies (hagiographies) in that factual material is mixed with faith statements and interpretations. C. H. Dodd states the problem this way: "All four gospels represent a tension between fact and interpretation."[28] Gunther Bornkamm indicates more precisely the difficulty in trying to give a historical account of the man Jesus: "To the original Christian tradition, Jesus is not in the first instance a figure of the past, but rather the risen Lord."[29]

The ambiguities caused by trying to sort out the teachings and actions of Jesus from the interpretations placed upon his actions and words by his early disciples do not deter scholars from making such attempts. In one such effort to sort out the man Jesus from the Christ of faith, C. H. Dodd suggests some probable personality traits of Jesus.[30] First of all, Dodd suggests that Jesus' *uniqueness* shows through the originality of some of his teachings (e.g., love not just your neighbor, but your enemy also—see Matt. 5:43-44 and Luke 6:27, 35). Second, Dodd says that Jesus was a man "*with a mind of a poetic and imaginative cast.*" For example, Jesus' teachings were cast in apocalyptic imagery (heavenly banquet) and story forms (parables) meant to reach the common people. Third, Jesus appeared to be *interested* in all classes and races of people. He dined with tax collectors, touched lepers, counseled prostitutes. Fourth, through his interest in people Jesus exhibited *compassion, sympathy,* and a *strength of character* necessary to stand up to, yet not hate, those religious leaders who had failed their calling by his standard. Fifth, Jesus was a man of uncommon *authority* who could claim to fulfill the teachings of the Jewish laws and prophets (e.g., "You have heard it said . . . but I say to you" in the Sermon on the Mount, Matt. 5:27-44). He spoke and acted with an authority that could only be described as "from the Father"—i.e., God (Matt. 11:27).

Bornkamm is less certain than Dodd of the possibility of separating the man Jesus from the Christ of faith in the Gospel accounts of Jesus. What we can say with some assurance, according to Bornkamm, is that Jesus was reared in Galilee in a Jewish family of a carpenter named Joseph. Jesus likely had brothers and sisters. The family's mother tongue was Aramaic (a dialect of Hebrew). His baptism by John the Baptist marked the beginning of Jesus' public career of teaching, healing, and traveling among the people of Palestine. His public ministry was approximately three years in duration and was marked by continual debates and conflicts with Jewish leaders, especially the Pharisees and Sadducees. Finally, his last conflict with the political and religious authorities occurred in Jerusalem, where he was eventually crucified.[31]

Bornkamm agrees with Dodd that a special authority is granted to the person and teachings of Jesus in the Gospels but indicates that such an attribution is bound up in the experience of those already submissive to that authority. Therefore, no clear picture of what Jesus perceived himself to be arises. What does emerge, however, is a picture of the disciples' interpretation of Jesus and his mission. The early oral traditions that inform the Gospels agree when expressing the core teaching of Jesus to be, "Repent, and believe in the Gospel" (Mark 1:14) or "Repent, for the kingdom of heaven is at hand" (Matt. 4:17). Bornkamm concurs with the notion that Jesus' message was a simple one: God's kingdom is near, so one should prepare for it. A further explication of this central teaching can be found in chapter 13 of Matthew, where parables or stories are devoted to the nature and centrality of God's rule in the lives of humans, which is expressed as the kingdom of heaven or kingdom of God. The basic conviction of Jesus was simply "that God will reign." Moreover, in the Synoptic reports the assertion is made that the kingdom of God already has come in the person and authority of the man Jesus (e.g., Luke 11:20 and 17:20ff). Yet, a sense of urgency filled the command of Jesus to repent ("turn about") and believe, which implies that the Jewish eschatological hope of a heavenly kingdom beyond this world was likely shared in some form by Jesus. Bornkamm concurs when he says that both emphases—of a present and future reign of God—are present in the teachings of Jesus.

In spite of what we can know of the person and message of Jesus, any attempts to describe accurately the personality of the historical Jesus are bound in the end to be frustrated. For what was crucial to the early disciples was the sacredness of the message and person of Jesus. Jesus was, for his early followers, the awaited Messiah, the Son of God, the promised messenger of the immanent kingdom (e.g., Matt. 16:13-16; John 6:69 and 11:27; Acts 9:20). Not without overlap and ambiguity, Jesus was understood to be the awaited Davidic King (e.g., Mark 11:10; 15:26; Matt. 27:37-43), Isaiah's suffering servant (e.g., Matt. 26:67-68; 27:27-31; Acts 8:32-33), and the apocalyptic Son of man (e.g., Matt. 14:21-25). His message proclaimed the advent of the awaited kingdom of God—"The time is fulfilled, and the kingdom of God is at hand" (Mark 1:15). Regardless of Jesus' own view of himself and his message, it is in the experience of those early followers who traveled with him when he was alive and experienced a tragic loss at his death that the Christian fellowship had its beginning.[32] The Synoptic records, therefore, lend valuable assistance when the experiences of the followers are the subject under investigation. That is, it is possible the man Jesus *was* as compassionate and sympathetic as the Gospel accounts indicate, but what is of paramount importance to the early Christian fellowship is that the early disciples *experienced* Jesus as loving and compassionate.

The disciples' experience of Jesus gave rise to their belief that he was a god-man. Christian scriptures point to countless experiences that indicate, *for the writers*, the divinity of the man Jesus.[33] Therefore, the debate is misplaced that argues about Jesus' sacred nature or birth. For the early disciples, miraculous or compassionate events were the signs that demonstrated the sacred character of Jesus. Furthermore, Jesus' death was the crucial event-experience for his disciples that codified for them all their earlier convictions.

Both C. H. Dodd and Rudolf Bultmann treat the death and resurrection of Jesus as the central belief of the early Christian community. Dodd says that the central belief of the early Christians was that Jesus rose from the dead.[34] Rudolf Bultmann places the disciples' experience of Jesus' death *and* resurrection in the context of the apocalyptic hope for a redeemer who will usher in the new age.[35] Consequently, if anything can be said with certainty about the assertions of the early disciples, it is that they *claim an experience of the presence* of Jesus *after his death.* Bornkamm puts it this way: "The last historical fact . . . is the Easter faith of the disciples."[36] Perhaps the empty-tomb stories have as one goal the proving to outsiders of this miraculous experience (see Mark 16:1-7; Luke 24:1-9; Matt. 28:1-8). Perhaps the appearance stories (e.g., at Galilee in Matt. 28:16-20, or to the disciples on the Emmaus Road in Luke 24:13-31) have as one of their purposes the chastisement of unbelievers for their unbelief, and the encouragement of others to persist in their fledgling faith (Mark 16:14). What these story traditions reveal most clearly is the fact that the disciples who admired and followed Jesus during his short ministry and became disheartened and disowned him at his death (e.g., Mark 14:66-72 and Luke 23:27, 48-49) later proclaimed his presence among them. Bornkamm says that whatever the differences in traditions and views among the disciples and other laymen, the claim to an experience of Jesus after his death was "not the particular experience of a few enthusiasts . . . they are all united in believing and acknowledging the risen Lord."[37]

A particularly dramatic description of a post-resurrection experience of Jesus was Saul of Tarsus' encounter on the road to Damascus (Acts 9:1-19). It is hard, without granting some type of immediate experience, to explain why Saul of Tarsus (Paul), who was a persecutor of Christians, became an avid Christian himself. Paul seemed to be a man on fire, a person energized not simply to reverse a mental conviction but actively to live, to preach, and to teach his new religion. Laing's overstatement makes the point: "Paul of Tarsus was picked up by the scruff of the neck, thrown to the ground and blinded for three days. This direct experience was self-validating."[38]

Another important occurrence for the early church was that event commonly called the Pentecost experience (Acts 2:1-41). At a large gathering of disciples and many curiosity seekers shortly after the death of Jesus, some experience occurred that was described as a "tongue of fire" from heaven that caused each person present to "speak in tongues" (i.e., a glossolalic experience). Paul later suggests that such holy gibberish may be the sign of deep experience or "possession" by God but is of little value for nonbelievers, who cannot understand it. He says, "I thank God that I speak in tongues more than you all; nevertheless, in church I would rather speak five words with my mind, in order to instruct others, than ten thousand words in a tongue" (I Cor. 14:18-19). Yet the very necessity for Paul to chastise those possessed of the "spirit" indicates the continuing presence of experiences similar to that described on Pentecost.

It seems clear that the early disciples experienced events during Jesus' life and after his death that convinced them he was the Son of God, the Sacred come to earth. The early Christian experience—later explicated as "belief"—was of a man-god named Jesus, whose life was identified and characterized by love, grace, and judgment. The disciples' reasons for this characterization were their experiences related to the man Jesus.

What is most puzzling to the non-initiate is that the core experiences of the early Christians apparently occurred after Jesus' crucifixion. Therefore, we find the central emphasis placed on the resurrection by early Christians. Paul, perhaps, best summarized this fact: "If Christ has not been raised, your faith is futile" (I Cor. 15:17). Perhaps this feature of the experience of early Christians explains why Jesus' life and ministry became crucially important only *after* his death. This is noted in the disproportionate amount of oral and written tradition that focuses upon the last week of his life (nearly one third of the Gospel accounts) and the complete absence of a birth narrative in all but two of the New Testament documents (Matthew and Luke). Furthermore, since his ministry of approximately three years formed the abiding experience of Jesus by the early disciples, the remaining two thirds of the Gospel accounts report those years *from the perspective of a Lord already risen.* For example, prophecies of his impending death are written back into his sacred history again and again (e.g., Matt. 12:14; 26:31-35; Mark 10:32-34; Luke 9:18-22; John 7:25-31).

Therefore, the resurrection experience is the controlling experience of the disciples by which all other, even earlier, events are interpreted.[39] Whether or not Jesus was raised from his grave is not open either to historical or to scientific investigation. What is clear is that the early Christians claimed to experience Jesus' presence beyond his death. Furthermore, such experiences were responsible for the rise of the early Christian community. In more partisan language, Bornkamm asserts, "The church has its origin and its beginning in the resurrection of Jesus Christ . . . the governing factor in this origin and beginning."[40] To experience the man Jesus was to experience God himself (e.g., Matt. 11:27; John 1:14; 16:27-28). Thus, the experience of many early Christians is well summarized by the Fourth Evangelist: "No one has ever seen God; the only Son, who is in the bosom of the Father, he has made him known" (John 1:18).

Siddhārtha Becomes the Buddha

Historically, the rise of Indian Buddhism in situated halfway between the Exodus of Moses' tribes and the birth of Jesus. Siddhārtha Gautama, the man later known as the Buddha, lived and taught in the sixth century B.C. (c. 560–480 B.C.).[41] The geographical location of the life and work of Gautama was the northeastern end of the Indo-Gangetic plain contained in the contemporary countries of Nepal and India. Madhyadeśa, or "middle country," was its name. In the sixth century B.C., many city-states (monarchies and republics) vied for political control of the fertile lands and commercial trade routes in Madhyadeśa. The rival kingdoms of Magadha and Kośala, with their respective capitals of Rājagraha and Śrāvasta, were the two most powerful kingdoms of Siddhārtha's day. Kapilavastu was the major city of the small state called Śākhya, which was nestled against the Himalayan foothills east of Kośala and north of Magadha. It was within the political confines of Śākhya that Siddhārtha was said to have been born.[42]

The cities of Siddhārtha's day were the centers of commerce and military control, as well as the focus of dramatic, literary, and religious activity. Compared with the rural villages whose life-style had been dominant the century before, the major and middle-sized cities of the sixth century B.C. offered a life more cosmopolitan. There were various areas of the city set aside for sports, literary instruction, dramatic productions, and religious debates. Kings and wealthy merchants were proud patrons of artistic and religious leaders. (One of the first converts of the Buddha is said to have been Bimbisāra, the King of Magadha.) Therefore, a pattern common to many religious traditions of the day was one in which wealthy merchants or kings gave material support to those identified as great religious teachers, while lively public debates and ethical discourses were the reciprocal contribution of the sages. City life also included the ancient professions of thievery, prostitution, and gambling and therefore was deemed inferior to the more simple rural life by some religious texts such as the *Arthaśāstra*.[43] Caste was an accepted social structure and regulated most aspects of life, from the food that could be eaten to the persons whom one could marry. Occupational guilds also reflected the caste structure in which a young man was obliged to enter the trade or profession of his father. Socially and intellectually, the cities were places of experimentation. Unlike Jesus, who carried his message to the rural villages and people of Palestine, the religious leaders of Siddhārtha's time focused their ministries on the developing urban settlements of the Madhyadeśa.

The intellectual and religious milieu of sixth-century B.C. Magadha and environs included two conflicting paths to salvation. One influential intellectual tradition was that of the Vedic Aryans. The second was that of the indigenous ascetic mendicants. The Aryans were a people foreign to India who had swept across the north of India from the west, beginning in the fifteenth or sixteenth century B.C. These pastoral seminomads brought with them a religious culture that held the sacrifice as its central religious activity, and gods representing natural forces (wind, fire, etc.) and social necessities (war, contracts, etc.) as the receivers of the sacrifice.[44] Besides the primary gods, popular belief included many lesser gods, heavenly musicians, tree and water nymphs, and demonic dwarfs and giants. The central Aryan ritual practice, the sacrifice, was performed on a temporary altar constructed on a public site made holy with prayers and ritual cleansing, or in a home where the father was the priest. Both public and private sacrifices perceived and personalized fire (Agni) as an emissary of the gods. The religious traditions of the Aryans were contained in four collections of hymns, called the Vedas. By the time of the Buddha, the Vedic priests, called *brāhmaṇas*, had developed sacrificial texts (Brāhmaṇas), which explicated in minute detail the action and intent of all the sacrifices, public and private. The crucial place of the sacrifice for Vedic religion is noted by one commentator, who says:

Future existence, at least of a blessed character, is assured to a man only through the correct performance of sacrifice. The sacrificer is reborn after death from the fire into the midst of the gods and enjoys an immortal existence imagined after the manner of the life here [on earth].[45]

However, the positive and pleasurable world view of the Vedic Aryans was not accepted by all members of that community. By the sixth century B.C., some of the *brāhmaṇas* had adopted an ascetic and mendicant life-style closely resembling the non-Aryan indigenous mendicants called *śramaṇas*.[46] Perhaps it was the result of the overritualization of the sacrifice or the social disruption of developing urban life, but whatever the cause, a negative assessment of the world and its pleasures began to creep into the *brāhmaṇas'* interpetations of their sacrificial religion. The end product was a reflective series of writings called Upaniṣads, which represented initially a reinterpretation of the sacrifice in cosmic terms, but finally, a negation of the very world enriched by the sacrifice.[47] The three concepts that arose as interdependent explanations of the unfortunate condition of all living beings were *saṃsāra, karma,* and *dharma.* While there are many stages to their development, and multiple uses of these concepts by different sages within and without the Vedic traditions, a general definition of each will serve as an indication of the intellectual milieu in which Siddhārtha began his quest for salvation.

The word *saṃsāra* literally means "going or wandering through," but the concept refers usually to the transmigration of souls or life-monads (*ātman* or *puruṣa*) through countless births and deaths.[48] Therefore, *saṃsāra* is perceived as the temporal and material cycle of rebirth in which all sentient beings are caught up. This concept of cyclical time is not restricted to the human domain only, but includes all the occupants of the hells and heavens as well as the material cosmos itself. Consequently, from the saṃsāric perspective the whole universe (including the Vedic gods themselves) are in a constant process of decay leading up to the next periodic dissolution of the whole cosmos. Such a perception of time and human condition is not a neutral one, but rather is loaded with pessimistic overtones for anyone who would value his or her

44

phenomenal existence. One of the later Upaniṣads indicates the extent of worldly rejection *saṃsāra* notions represent to the earlier, empirically oriented Vedic sacrificial cults:

> Sir, in this ill-smelling, unsubstantial body, which is a conglomerate of bone, skin, muscle, marrow, flesh, semen, blood, mucus, tears, rheum, fecus, urine, wind, bile, and phlegm, what is the good of enjoyment of desires? . . . We see that this whole world is decaying, as these gnats, mosquitoes, and the like, the grass, and the trees that arise and perish. . . . In this sort of cycle of existence *saṃsāra)* what is the good of enjoyment of desires, when after a man has fed on them there is seen repeatedly his return here to earth?[49]

Even the Lord of the Vedic gods, Indra, is subject to periodic deaths and rebirths.[50] Rebirth is not thought to be simply a matter of chance, however, but is explained by the notions of *karma* and *dharma*. That is, the notions of *karma* and *dharma* account for the favored or despised condition of all those born in the world, whether king or priest, wealthy landlord or poor slave.

Karma refers to what one does *and* to the residual effects or "fruits" of action. Whatever a person (or other living being) does is judged to have good or bad "effects," which accumulate over a lifetime and determine the status, quality, and length of both this and the next life in *saṃsāra*. One of the earliest Upaniṣads summarized the law of *karma* this way: "According as one acts, according as one conducts himself, so does he become. The doer of good becomes good. The doer of evil becomes evil. One becomes virtuous by virtuous action, bad by bad action."[51] What determines an action to be good or bad is its relationship to the actor's duty, or *dharma*. Each person, by virtue of his or her caste, sex, and stage of life, has certain prescribed duties or dharmic responsibilities. For example, the Taittiriya Upaniṣad rehearses the instruction a teacher (brāhmaṇa) gives to a student:

> Speak the truth. Practice virtue (dharma). Neglect not
> the study [of the Vedas, including the Upaniṣads] . . .
> One should not be negligent of truth.
> One should not be negligent of virtue.
> One should not be negligent of welfare.
> One should not be negligent of prosperity.
> One should not be negligent of study and teaching.
>
> One should not be negligent of duties to the gods and
> to the fathers.
> Be one to whom a mother is as a god.
> Be one to whom a father is as a god.
> Be one to whom a teacher is as a god.
> Be one to whom a guest is as a god.[52]

As the notions of karma and dharma became more refined, whole texts, such as the Laws of Manu, were written to explicate the dharma of a caste (from warriors to serfs), a profession (from teachers to prostitutes), a social position (from kings to wives), or a stage of life (student, householder, or ascetic).[53]

The pessimistic world view represented by saṃsāra, attended by dharmic regulations and karmic effects, is most likely the result of the influence of indigenous ascetics and their ideas upon the reflective brāhmaṇas who wrote the Upaniṣads. The indigenous ascetics and their ideas, then, represent the second major intellectual and social influence in the cultural milieu in which Buddhism arose.

In the early days of the Aryan incursion (c. 1500–1000 B.C.) into the northeast of the Indian subcontinent, the Vedic priests wrote about one group of "ecstatic sages," called munis, that intersected their community.[54] These wandering ascetics had long, matted hair, wore soiled yellow robes, and were recognized for their emotional flights of mind. They claimed to be ones into whom the gods entered. The munis proclaimed, "In the intoxication of ecstacy, we are mounted on the winds. You mortals can only see our body."[55] The munis were friends with Vayu, the Wind, and could fly through the air and inhabit the land of the rising and setting suns (i.e., lands of birth and death). They could drink poison, read thoughts, and defy most natural laws. A similarly perplexing mendicant group of the early Vedic times was made up of vrātyas, or "low, vile persons."[56] These sages wore turbans or had shaved heads, dressed in black, and carried a staff and an unstrung bow. These persons practiced extreme asceticism grounded in the belief that to cleanse one's body was to purify the very cosmos itself. The ideas and ideals of the vrātyas were repugnant to the Vedic cults (such that the very presence of a vrātya would vitiate a performance of the Vedic sacrifice). G. C. Pande remarks concerning these mendicant ascetics, "Thus we can discern in the Vedic period, outside the strictly Vedic pale, wandering groups of ascetics sometimes styled as Munis who were 'the precursors of the strange ascetics of later India.'"[57] Still, the influence of such mendicant groups upon Vedic thought and practices was great.

By the sixth century B.C., the general name given to the indigenous mendicant ascetics was śramaṇa or "the one who makes an effort or becomes weary."[58] The śramaṇas, clad in variously colored robes or no clothes at all, traveled about begging for food. They were persons who had rejected caste, or, more properly, who perceived themselves to be beyond caste, and were noted for their austere and ascetic life-styles. Those who gathered themselves around a teacher and wandered about searching for the perfect wisdom were called parivrājakas.[59] As representatives of a world view opposed to the Vedic sacrificial notions, their basic religious drive stemmed from their ascetic pessimism. Pande summarizes the teachings of the *śramaṇa* groups with the adjectives "ascetic, atheistic, pluralistic and 'realistic.'"[60] Believing the world to be dualistically composed of matter and spirit, the ascetics utilized austere techniques for controlling the body and freeing the spirit. The source of ultimate truth, therefore, was thought to be the freed, nonmaterial self, not any deity. It is not surprising, then, that the notion of *saṃsāra* and its negative assessment of worldly life are usually considered indigenous contributions to the Upaniṣadic *brāhmaṇas*.[61] It was in this religiously alive world of the sixth century B.C. that Buddhism arose as another challenge to the Aryan world upheld and enriched by the Vedic sacrifice.

The earliest Buddhist texts surprisingly do not reveal much attempt at all at a biography of the man destined to become the Buddha, yet several main features of Siddhārtha's life stand out as very likely events, even in the earliest oral traditions. One text, the Mahāparinibbāna Sutta, does give a connected account of the last days of Gautama's life and a recounting of his final release *(parinirvāṇa)*. While the Buddha most likely spoke the language of Magadha *(māgadhī)*, the bulk of the extant texts are written in a literary dialect known as Pāli.[62] Therefore, the canonized scriptures of the early Buddhist monks, called Theras or "Elders," are referred to as the Pāli Canon, or the Tripiṭaka (Pāli, *Tripiṭaka*—"Three Baskets"). Just as the Hebrew and Christian scriptures were not written by one person, so also the Tripiṭaka developed out of many oral traditions representing numerous authors and redactors.[63] Yet in spite of the textual difficulties, Richard H. Drummond, who utilizes the earliest strata of the Pāli scriptures, says it is possible to construct a "portrait of the Buddha which is both

coherent and essentially faithful to the historical data."[64]
It is such a brief historical sketch that will be presented.

Much like the early Christians, the followers of the
Buddha appear to have become interested in the early life
of Gautama only after his death. Moreover, a consistent
deterrent to interest in the earlier history of the person
Gautama was the Buddha's insistence that each person
must tread the path to liberation using only himself or
herself as a guide.[65] Consequently, the Buddha was
considered by the early monastic community as a man
who had *found* the path, but who *was not himself* the
path.[66] What does survive as possibly a reliable account of
the life of Gautama is the following:[67] He was born near
Kapilavastu in Śākhya country of the family of Suddhodana and likely led the privileged life of the ruling
class. At the age of twenty-nine, Gautama renounced the
relative luxury of his father's home and set out in search of
spiritual satisfaction.[68] For a period of six or seven years,
Gautama tried various avenues to enlightenment. First, he
successively joined two wandering teachers (Ārāda
Kālāma of Vaiśālī and Udraka Rāmaputra of Magadha). He
learned their teachings (dharma), lived under their rules
of discipline (vinaya), and was a member of their religious
order (saṅgha).[69] Gautama decided that neither of his
teachers could provide the highest level of mental
awareness.[70] Leaving the learned debates and speculations to others, Gautama next tried the extremely ascetic
techniques made famous by mendicant groups such as the
Jains. The severity of Gautama's austerities (the most
notable of which was a long period of fasting) attracted to
him five disciples who eagerly awaited a breakthrough by
their new master. Apparently no such dramatic event
occurred, except Gautama's near demise. At that point,
Gautama rejected ascetic practices as a way to salvation,
and his disciples are said to have left in disgust over the

failure of their leader. It was at that time that Gautama resorted to the techniques of *jhñāna* or meditation. And it was this third route that finally proved fruitful, since through meditation the Śākhyan prince became the Buddha, the Enlightened One.

Drummond says of Gautama's enlightenment experience, "There can be no doubt that the experience was vitally real for him and decisive for his subsequent career and teaching." The exact character of the Buddha's experience is not easily recovered because of the stylized recounting of it by his followers. The Dīgha Nikāya No. 22 lists four stages of awareness and three degrees of knowledge in the enlightenment of the Buddha.[71] According to this tradition, Gautama's first stage of mental awareness was marked by rapture and detachment from worldly sensations, yet discursive thought remained. The second stage of consciousness was characterized by concentration and the lack of discursive thought. The third stage of mental progress included an equanimity or calmness combined with alertness. The fourth and final stage of mental disposition was marked by the absence of pleasure or sorrow, rapture or anguish. All activity of the mind had ceased, and "pure mindfulness" alone remained. *Nirvāṇa* had been achieved.

So conditioned by the process of meditation and in a particularly alert state of mind, Gautama is said to have obtained three degrees of knowledge, one during each of the three watches of the night. The first acquisition was knowledge of all his previous births. The second watch of the night afforded a glimpse into the agitation and flux *(anitya)* that permeate all material reality. It was in this period of the night that the Buddha perceived directly the chain of existence in which all living beings are caught in endless rebirths. During the last hours of the night, the Buddha is said to have discovered the four noble truths (i.e., the true nature of life and the path to escape from such suffering). The first and basic truth is that worldly life is filled with suffering (duhkha). The remaining truths name the cause of suffering (attachment and craving), proclaim the end of suffering (cease craving), and indicate the path that can eradicate craving (the eightfold path leading to an experience like that of the Buddha). The Majjima Nikāya I. 4. 21-23 records the Buddha saying of his enlightenment:

> I am freed; and I comprehended: Destroyed is birth, brought to a close is the Brahma-faring (the doing of what is right), done is what was to be done, there is no more of being such or such . . . ignorance was dispelled, knowledge arose, darkness was dispelled, light arose even as I abided diligent, ardent, self-resolute.[72]

According to the early texts, Buddha saw all his teachings as originating in his climactic experience. Therefore, while the Buddha's dharma, or moral way, could be expressed to some extent in available language and categories, full realization of them could only be acquired through direct experience of Nirvāna. The sacred truth, which is known only through experience, was said to be

> profound, difficult to realize, hard to understand, tranquilliz-ing, sweet, not to be grasped by mere logic, subtle, comprehensible only by the wise, which the Tathāgata [i.e., "the one who crossed over," the Buddha], having himself realized and seen face to face, hath set forth.[73]

While the fourfold stages of meditation and the threefold bodies of knowledge are most likely later systematizations of the teachings of the monkish community, there is general agreement that the two notions of anitya and duhkha were the products of Buddha's own experience.[74]

Understood by worldly standards, the notion of the impermanence of the world (Pāli: *anicca*) and the claim that all of life is characterized by suffering (Pāli: *dukkha*) seem to be pessimistic and negative results of the enlightenment experience. The other side of Buddha's experience, however, was marked by calmness and a liberation from the transient life of the world. This state of mind (and, perhaps, state of being) is called *Nirvāṇa* (Pāli: *nibbāna*). But because of the impossibility of conceptualizing and talking about *Nirvāṇa*, the Buddha stressed, instead, human suffering and the way out of the transient, suffering world of *saṃsāra*.[75] His own decision to return from the pinnacle of his religious experience to teach others the path by which he had attained his vision of reality and experience of liberation is understood by the early community as the essential sign of Buddha's compassion *(karuṇa)* for all living beings.[76]

Much must remain unsaid here about the legend associated with the early life and teachings attributed to the Buddha. However, the central feature of the Buddha's life for subsequent generations was his immediate and intuitive experience of *Nirvāṇa* (sacred calm) and the path to liberation he founded. Having rejected both the way of pleasure and comfort and the opposite extreme of ascetic austerity, the Buddha developed a *dhamma*, or set of teachings, which was accepted by his followers as the Middle Way. Buddha's *dhamma* was grounded in his climactic experience, which suggested that *all* attachment to the world (love or hate, grasping or indifference) leads to suffering *(duḥkha)*. As long as the material and human worlds are by their very nature in constant flux and agitation *(anitya)*, only cessation of craving and desiring can lead to a state of liberated calm *(Nirvāṇa)*. The route the Buddha traveled to the cessation of desire was *jhñāna* (Pāli: *jhāna*) or meditation. Further, it was in the elevated calm of Nirvāṇa that the teachings of the Buddha were spawned. Buddha's experience of the Sacred Reality of Nirvāṇa led him to teach "that Saṃsāra is dukkha, Nirvāṇa is peace ineffable, the Mārga ["Path"] is primarily Jhānic practice."[77]

Summary Comment

The evidence just cited demonstrates the experiential nature of the rise and development of religious traditions. The conclusion of Laing that people first experience a Sacred Power (which he calls God) before they believe in one seems justified. Although all encounters with Sacred Power do not fit one experiential pattern or assert equivalent characteristics of the Sacred, they all do provide the starting point of their respective religious traditions. Such originative religious experiences do not occur in cultures devoid of religious ideas and institutions; yet their effect is to create a new awareness of a Power not previously or personally known. One similarity, then, between the early Semitic, Christian, and Buddhist communities is their formation out of experiences of a Sacred Power. Consequently, one sacred world is the mode of living and understanding generated by religious experience. Personal religiosity, therefore, is a life begun and lived out of an apprehension of a Sacred Power.

The dissimilarities of the origination of the traditions illustrated include the nature and content of the religious experiences. The Hebrew people experienced Yahweh cumulatively in events of nature and history associated with their Exodus journey. The early followers of Jesus experienced the love and power of their God immediately, though indirectly, through experiences of the risen Jesus (a mediator). The Buddha, however, immediately and directly experienced the potency of Nirvāṇa, an eternal calm. The second dissimilarity is the description of the Sacred Power experienced in each tradition. The Hebrews and Christians affirm a relationship to an active, personal god, whereas the Buddha insisted that *Nirvāṇa* was an impersonal and amorphous Reality that was "deep and difficult to describe." These differences of terminology and conception can be explained, to some extent, by the cultural milieu in which experiences of the Sacred occurred. Therefore, it is to a second sacred realm, created and controlled by social processes and institutions, that we shall now turn.

Chapter 2
The Religion of
Social Experience

Thesis

A second sacred world, and the one in which most religious persons live, is that realm of religious awareness which originates in the processes of socialization. I will designate this type of sacred standpoint "social religion" because its inauguration depends upon a socialization process wider in scope and participants than a single religious institution. Still, religious institutions and organizations are the usual focus of this kind of religiosity, even when the socialization process includes the family, social peers, or the community as a whole (e.g., a person being raised in a Hare Krishna community). In any case, I intend to focus on one theoretical understanding of the forces that influence the social integration of persons into religious awareness, and to leave to trained sociologists a full description of the religious institution's role in what William James called derogatorily "second-hand" religion. In so doing, it would be my hope that the vitality and comprehensiveness of social religion might be appreciated without James' comparative bias.

Social Realities and Religion

A straightforward, though dated, explanation of religion as a social phenomenon comes from the pen of the French sociologist Emile Durkheim. The heart of his message is, "If religion has given birth to all that is essential in society, it is because the idea of society is the soul of religion. Religious forces are therefore human forces, moral forces."[1] Peter Berger and Thomas Luckmann, two contemporary sociologists of religion, approach their analysis of religion as a socially created "world" with the assertion that *all* "realities" are socially constructed.[2] These two sociologists begin their argument by defining as "real" those phenomena which are perceived to exist independent of human volition. Knowledge, then, is the certainty that these phenomena are real and have describable characteristics. For example, the commonsense "world" of everyday life is a reality accepted by most persons, although what is known to be "true" is variously constituted in different cultures, societies, or subsocieties. The phenomena in it are arranged in patterns intelligible even to the uneducated. Within this here-and-now realm, geographical location, vocational status, family relationships, and the manufactured environment (from toothbrushes to computers) are intelligible to most laypersons. Consequently, all the elements of the everyday world are givens that "are taken for granted as reality."[3] There are other realms or realities (e.g., the realms of biological research, of dreams, or of religious behavior and belief) in which a person consciously operates. Nonetheless, among the multiple realities, that of the everyday is the paramount reality.[4]

A necessary assumption for Berger and Luckmann's sociology of knowledge is that human knowledge exists in a society prior to individual experience and provides that experience with its order of meaning.[5] An application of this assumption leads Berger and Luckmann to concern themselves with the way in which societies construct their realities according to social processes. Consequently, their understanding of religion as a socially created phenomenon is consistent with their approach to any meaningful body of knowledge. If what a person takes to be real in the commonsense everyday world is influenced by what society teaches to be real, then it follows that religious realities also will bear the marks of their social setting.[6]

Peter Berger, in *The Sacred Canopy*, recognizes the dialectical or reciprocal relationship between human beings and their social environment (*i.e.*, society). He says, "Society is a product of man. . . . Yet it may also be stated that man is a product of society." This reciprocal relationship may be viewed as a circular process entailing externalization, objectification, and internalization.[7] Persons create mental (e.g., concepts, relationships, and language) and physical (e.g., spaceships, electric bulbs, and toilet paper) "outpourings," which when objectified become a particular society's culture, its reality. Once these human products are taken for granted as part and parcel of everyday reality (*i.e.*, they are objectified), they constitute the "facts" and the certain "knowledge" imparted to other members of society culminating in the process of internalization, a final stage in socialization.

Language plays a crucial role in all three phases of this reciprocal process because it serves as the primary vehicle of communication between members of a society and translates "raw" experiences into socially understood categories and concepts. Rooted in everyday life, language expresses feelings and conceptions (externalization); names ideas, objects, and events (objectification); and finally, by imposing differentiation and structure upon experiences, facilitates the "for me" quality of what is taught in the socialization of the young or uninitiated (internalization). Berger says, "Man invents a language and then finds that both his speaking and thinking are dominated by its grammar." The circle is completed when persons who generate ideas or elements of their environment are then controlled by them in that what began as self-expression now is understood as a "given," as reality itself. From this perspective, it is possible to explain the Muslim concept of "holy war" as the imposition on experience of culturally fabricated concepts (Allah and absolute obedience to him—*jihad*) that, when internalized, seem externally initiated and ultimately real. Only persons who have internalized (*i.e.*, been fully socialized into) such a socially created world will feel impelled to act in submission to Allah. Devotees of the Buddha hardly would rally to the cry for *jihad* or submission to Allah. At each stage in the reciprocal process leading to socialization, then, language is a key factor.

Created in the reciprocal human-social-human processes are worlds of meaning or multiple realities in which patterns of relationship are established and constituent elements are accepted as true or factual. Technical, and sometimes private, language guards the parameters of each specialized reality. Chemistry is one such socially created sphere of meaning. Religion is another. Socialization, then, is the thoroughgoing and persistent introduction of a person into one or more accepted realities of a society.[8] This process involves both cognitive learning (*e.g.*, of language, concepts, etc.) and emotional attachment (*e.g.*, a child's desire to "be like mommy" or a student's desire to "be a doctor").[9] Socialization as an internalizing process offers facts (objective reality, what is real "out there") to be accepted as *really* real (subjective reality, what is real for me). For example, the law of gravity as an accepted fact of science may be internalized by me so that I will cross the street to avoid possible falling objects as a new building is being constructed. I do not wonder if it is possible for objects to fall; I *know* that it is. Within a different sphere, my religion may teach that persons truly living in God's presence will not be affected by poisonous snakes. Handling such snakes fearlessly is a sign that I have internalized my religious conceptions, *i.e.*, that the socialization process was effectual.

Both the preceding examples are instances of the internalization of institutional "sub-worlds," or specialized realities. An even more elemental socialization is that childhood process by which more general social norms and traditions are imparted.[10] Therefore, in the acquisition of a social religious reality, cultural norms and sanctions are often included as a part of the institutional and familial socialization processes. Such an inclusion is especially likely when the socially accepted everyday reality is construed to be consistent with religious reality (e.g., socialization in a Muslim country or in ancient Israel). There are many places where internalization of social or religious realities may occur. But very often the central place of such activity, especially if it entails one of the sub-worlds like science or religion, is in a formal institution (e.g., school or church/temple respectively).

One way of viewing institutions is to see them as the extension of the "habitualization" of activity.[11] Human activity of all types (sexual, religious, political, etc.) can be repeated and routinized. When repetition of behavior occurs, patterns of behavior may develop that economize effort and increase the predictability of results and responses. From one perspective, social institutions are the result of routinized behavior and the guardian of that normalized behavior. Therefore, religious institutions may be conceived as just one way human activity is regularized. Maslow laments this process, which he calls "familiarization," because "it makes it unnecessary to attend, to think, to feel, to live fully, to experience richly." [12] Regardless of Maslow's lament, human beings are habitual creatures. Therefore, what begins as a spontaneous religious community with unstructured sharing and interaction (*i.e.*, a religious movement) usually culminates in regularized, institutionalized activity (*i.e.*, a religious institution). Furthermore, tensions may exist between personal needs for community (as represented in a religious movement) and the regularized demands of a structured institution.

Victor Turner, a noted anthropologist, defines well the relationship between a relatively unstructured sense of community ("communitas") and the necessary but structured nature of society. [13] He sees communitas as the homogeneous comradeship among persons "suspended" in marginal situations (such as life-cycle rites or monastic communities) and in marginal groups, whether ritually or socially defined. The key to an experience of communitas is a leveling of social distinctions in relationships providing a brief limbo or "liminal" state in the midst of a ritual or the life of a people. Occasional occurrences of unstructured or anti-structure communitas are juxtaposed with longer periods of structured order and relationships in most societies. Therefore, any spontaneous communitas (*e.g.*, a religious movement) is doomed to structure and law. [14] Turner also speaks of normative and ideological communities (*i.e.*, religious institutions) that form to encapsulate communitas (anti-structure) in a structure. From this angle of vision, the move toward institutionalization may be a move from communitas to structure. [15] From another angle of vision, society as a whole may be viewed as a "dialectic process with successive phases of structure and communitas."[16]

As we saw with respect to language, religious (and other) institutions may be viewed as man-made products that, when objectified, exert control and influence on their makers. Who would have guessed, in the days when Christian worship was regularized as a "Sabbath" activity, that Sunday blue laws would be viewed as a restriction of the American freedom to buy? In another context the Hebrew definitions of reality, when institutionalized, controlled the diet, speech, and actions of those who previously had eaten pork, worshiped Baal, or engaged in prostitution. Social control of persons, therefore, is usually placed in the hands of institutions. The same circle noted earlier in reality construction occurs here (for institutions are concretizations of specialized realities): (1) humans produce institutions (externalization); (2) institutions react back on them (as an objective reality); and therefore (3) persons become, in one sense, institutional products (integrated). In short, reality is defined, tasks are assigned, and roles prescribed by institutions that persons create as an attempt to regularize their activity.

Control of human conduct and thought is, therefore, a primary function of a religious (or any) institution. But institutionalization leads to more than social control alone; it also provides a history of human activity over the span of generations. A basic, positive contribution that institutions make involves their providing for each succeeding generation the wisdom and "knowledge" of previous generations, i.e., preserving traditions. Consequently, a tradition may be viewed as the accumulated history and knowledge of an institution. Institutions arise at the end of a developmental process in which specific actions and actors are given prescribed meanings that are regularly repeated. When habitual actions or roles are granted the status of "facts" by a group of persons, institutionalization has arrived. Tradition is a recounting of the history of this whole process. It tells what the actions mean and who the actors are. It states the givens and usually explains them. Tradition, then, is the biographical memory of the founders of an institution that needs to be presented to new generations through socialization processes, both primary and secondary.

It is through a secondary socialization process Berger calls legitimation that individuals new to the institution become acquainted with its history and its defense. While legitimations will be discussed later in the framework of religious constructs and theology, it might be important to note here that what is at stake in the legitimation process is the very plausibility of a given world view as the ultimate reality. For example, if the notion of a male god (e.g., Yahweh of Judaism) is debunked as a sexist's conception created by a male-dominated society, legitimating answers have to be devised before the plausibility of Judaism can be shared by those making the accusations. Likewise, heretics often force the creation of legitimating formulas by those within the institution who wish to quell what they consider deviant behavior or thought (e.g., Manichaean heresy and resulting trinitarian formulas). Therefore, the central roles of religious tradition are to preserve the collective memory and history of a particular religious institution and to defend that institution and its knowledge from attack with legitimating formulas. Neither function of tradition is ever fully accomplished, since fresh events must always be incorporated into the institution's history and new legitimations created and added to the storehouse of specialized knowledge to maintain that religion's plausibility.

Social religion, therefore, is a second realm in which religious persons live. The socialization process that culminates in social religiosity involves most often what was earlier described as cumulative religious experience.[17] Few persons who have received their religiosity through the socialization process alone would claim immediate or direct experience of a sacred reality. Hence, persons who live in the world of social religion tend to describe their religion in terms of what they "believe," not what they know experientially (especially in Western religious traditions).[18] It would seem that, for the most part, experiences connected with social religion tend toward the rational end of the continuum, not the emotional. This observation does not mean that persons who have been converted by the "Word" will not defend it vociferously. Furthermore, such an assertion does not mean that such religion is a religion without experiences. Rather, the claim made is that the realm of social religion is one most dependent upon the socialization process (with its manifold secular experiences) rather than upon personal experiences of the sacred.

Put bluntly, social religion is a socially constructed reality. Society provides many realities for habitation by its members, and social religion may be just one of those realities. A religious reality is often one of the most important realities for a person because it deals with problem areas of experience not fully encompassed by other realities. Death is the most obvious example of a crisis situation that everyday reality finds difficult to address. Death contradicts an everyday reality which assumes the greatest value for carnal or physical existence. However, religious reality is better able to address such a crisis situation through its appeal to a cosmic view of life and to a spiritual or nonmaterial order of reality that transcends the human world containing the experiences of death and birth. On the other hand, the very willingness of most religious traditions to tackle the meaning of crisis situations (e.g., death, suffering, the origin of life), and to appeal to sacred mysteries, make their legitimations most vulnerable to attack from the position of commonsense, everyday reality. Nonetheless, whatever the depth of conviction, most persons who call themselves religious abide in a sacred world arising from social processes. Such persons commonly adopt the religion or nonreligion of their parents, accept what is comfortable or reasonable from their institution's offerings and demands, and seldom challenge their society's right to interpret what the moral implications (individually and collectively) of their religion include. This realm of religion is a sacred world and cannot be judged simply as a second-hand or inferior religious reality. For not only does this reality have the integrity brought about by social acceptance, but also it is linked, in an inseparable way, to the realm of personal religion. With this last statement I depart from Berger's sociological standpoint and urge a recognition of the interdependent connection between the two sacred worlds of personal and social religion.

Most psychologists recognize the interdependence of personal and social religion but eschew any comment of the "secondhand" world of the institution—except to deride it. William James notes:

> Churches, when once established, live at second-hand upon tradition; but the *founders* of every church owed their power originally to the fact of their direct personal communion with the divine. . . . So personal religion would still seem the primordial thing, even to those who continue to esteem it incomplete.[19]

In this same context, James defines religion as a product of religious experience (i.e., feelings and acts) out of which "theologies, philosophies, and ecclesiastical organizations may secondarily grow." He chooses to dismiss social religion as simply a secondary phenomenon. Certainly my previous analysis should suggest that for most religious persons, social religion comes *first* in their experience, not second. Most persons are socialized into their religion prior to, or exclusive of, any sense of the Sacred. Therefore, social religion has, for the generations not contemporary with the founders and their experience, a reality all its own.

Abraham Maslow appreciates the qualitative differences (while recognizing the interdependence) of the realms of social and personal religious awareness in his dichotomous grouping of prophets and organizers. The categories of prophets and organizers, or "legalists," are used to distinguish those founders who have had religious (peak) experiences from those persons who regulate, systematize, and organize religious behavior and proclamations in an institutional form.[20] The founders are prophets because they have peak experiences that, when shared, act as the creative nexus for institutionalization. From the point of view of the prophets (also called "lonely mystics" by Maslow), "each person has his own private religion . . . his own private myths and symbols, rituals and ceremonials."[21] The religious organizer, on the other hand, is usually a "non-peaker" who accepts the prophets' experiences as valid and normative. For him the ecclesiastical organization is the realm of faith, myths, symbols, etc. If it is the prophet who experiences a revelation of Sacred Power, it is the religious organizer who tries to make the revelation available to the masses. Therefore, the function of the religious institution is "to communicate peak-experiences to non-peakers."[22] The only problem is that very often the relationship between the prophet and the organizer is that between a "peaker and non-peaker!"

The prophet and the organizer, therefore, are two essentially different types of people who live in interdependent, though separate, realms of religiosity. The separateness of these modes of religious awareness is underscored when prophets accuse the organizers and their religious institution of *impeding* the acquisition of peak experiences by "religionizing" only one part of life (e.g., one day, one building, one person or "holy man").[23] By such a cornering of religion, institutions can gain power and prestige for themselves to the end that persons lose any sense of the Sacred not connected with their religious institution and its definitions of the Sacred.

What is important (in Maslow's observations) for my analysis is the recognition of the interdependence of the realms of personal religion and social religion. On the one hand, I would take to be obvious the primacy of personal religious experience(s) as the origin of any religious tradition. On the other hand, I recognize the essential needs and roles religious institutions fill for those of or those living beyond the founding generation. It may be that Hebrew religion arose out of the Exodus experience, but without Hebrew institutions that have included myth, ritual, judges, prophets, and priests, Hebrew religion would never have developed into the world religion known as Judaism. Likewise, without the formation of the *sangha* (assembly), Buddha's private enlightenment experience would not have been shared in countless forms with millions of people—monks and laymen—over the past twenty-five hundred years. Michael Novak states well the enigmatic, though necessary, relationship between personal and social religion. The conflict, as he sees it, is not between religious institutions and institutions of other realities that claim supremacy for their perspectives (e.g., political, economic, or philosophical). The real conflict, says Novak, is between the human spirit and *all* institutions, between the human spirit and its natural habitat. Institutions are the normal, natural expression of the human spirit. But that spirit is self-transcending. It is never satisfied with its own finite expressions.[24]

Two qualifications must now be made to the earlier descriptions of types of religious experience. Although it is the case that some persons acquire a religious reality through the gradual process of socialization, it is too pejorative *and* misleading to label these experiences secondhand. While socializing experiences (arising from religious services, parental instruction, priestly witness, etc.) are usually gradual and cumulative in nature, they differ from both cumulative and peak, or immediate, religious experiences in that they initiate the novice into a different realm of religious awareness, namely social religion. Institutional goals, demands, and priorities serve as the focus for social religiosity even when a Sacred Power is extolled as preeminent. For the sake of clarity, gradual socializing experiences will be called "social religious experience." A second differentiation that needs to be made in the context of social religion concerns the person who *does* have peak or immediate religious experiences within the context of his or her social religion. Those experiences which claim to repeat the originating experiences of the founder(s) I will call "confirming" or "codifying" religious experiences. For example, Martin Luther's dramatic experiences involving visions and natural signs (lightning) codified for him a Christian tradition already acquired through social religious experiences. Both social religious experiences and codifying religious experiences are usually cumulative in nature, but the essential difference is that the former includes no experiential sense of a Sacred Power.

One of the religious institution's primary functions is to provide occasions (especially in its rites, rituals, and worshiping activity) for confirming or codifying experiences. When such experiences occur, there is very often a shift in focus in the person thus motivated from institutional activity alone to concern for personal piety. Repeated experiences of the Sacred, rather than the more public demands of social religion, then take the fore. Codifying experiences, therefore, may confirm the received social religion to the extent that the social reality is subsequently perceived to be faithful to its originating impulse (that is, the experience of the founders). This confirmation may or may not include all the particular institutionalized creeds, dogmas, and ethics. In fact, it is often out of such confirming experiences of the Sacred Reality that prophets and iconoclasts are born. Such persons may claim that the institution has strayed from its founding experience.

While the main purpose of this study is to show the positive aspects of the interdependence of personal religious experiences and their social expressions, it should also be recognized that the relations between personal and social religiosity may be marked by conflict. For example, to fight and die for an Allah defined by and experienced through the social creeds and dogmas of the mosque has led many Muslims to participate in what they understood to be "holy wars" (jihad). On the other hand, to pray incessantly against war because submission to Allah (jihad) is experienced as requiring personal piety exemplified in love of others allows some sufis (Muslim mystics) to stand against the political expansion of Islam through warfare. In another context, the conflict Martin Luther had with institutional Christianity was, to a great extent, one of his personal religion's demanding a life of faith and service, which he felt the institutional church was actually thwarting with indulgences and other such hindrances to the growth of personal responsibility among the laity. Luther's personal religious awareness provided the grounds for his prophetic attack on the religious institution of which he claimed to be a part. Christianity, as personally conceived by Luther, was clearly at odds with the life of Christian obedience demanded by the highest institutional authority, the pope.

As Novak has noted, the basic conflict is between the human spirit and *all* institutions. No religious institution or tradition has escaped challenges to its creeds, dogmas, ethics, or authoritative proclamations from those who insist that the core experience of that same faith demands revisions of that institution's expressions of faith. Many reform movements, schisms, and new sects or denominations have arisen as the result of the clash of personal and social religiosity. Consequently, it is necessary to recognize that the roles of the prophet and the organizer (using Maslow's terms) are not always compatible and complementary but may, in fact, be at odds. It should also be apparent that the more a religious tradition reflects secular norms and attitudes, the more likely it is that defenders of personal piety will rise to question the institution's authority. It should also be obvious that those personal challenges themselves will often reflect social processes and attitudes. At the very least, personal religion participates in the language—and often the thought—of the very society it chooses to call into question.

Immediate religious experiences do not occur to persons who are void of previous socialization. Therefore, any person who receives an immediate religious experience brings to that experience the many realities into which he or she has already been socialized. The most obvious social tool is the language used to express even the most basic and profound religious experiences. To be sure, everyday language often fails to provide full expression of such experiences and therefore is used allegorically, symbolically, or metaphorically. Still, to the extent that persons are conditioned by their language and their society's realities, their immediate religious experiences are likewise conditioned. Even the mystic's experience, thought to be the most private and direct experience of the Divine, evidences its social context whenever the mystic chooses to speak. Furthermore, if the socialization processes have been effectual, the mystic may be bound by earlier formulations of religious institutions as to the nature of the Sacred encountered. This dependence is obvious when most Christian mystics "see" God as a male deity (usually Jesus), while a Hindu yogin may experience Śiva as androgynous and beyond all sexuality or as the primal Mother, Kālī.

To recognize the social effects that language and other social formulations bring to bear on immediate religious experience is not to imply that these influences may explain away whatever reality may lie behind those experiences as their author. It would seem that what the sociology of knowledge eventually does, in its most radical form, is to explain all thought and actions as consequences of social processes. Reality is, in this context, socially constructed. What I am suggesting is that most religious experiences necessitate articulation because of the very profound impact they have upon their receiver, and that it is the articulation that is most affected by social processes (*i.e.*, language). R. D. Laing argues that even the types and qualities of experiences available to persons—especially religious experiences—may be adversely affected by the socialization processes.[25] But his dire predictions concerning the effects of socialization overdraw the strength of social processes. The fact that sons and daughters are often radically different from their fathers and mothers is one example of the limits of socialization and the importance of personal qualities and experiences. Reformers, visionaries, and holy persons, all in some way, exhibit qualities and lives not fully conditioned by their societies' realities and institutions. Such observations lead some universalists to claim a *common* religious experience as the source of all deep religious experiences that are subsequently expressed in different cultural terms and languages.[26] The examples offered in this study suggest that the universalists' solution is a tough one to demonstrate, given the evidence of the world's religious traditions. If institutional ethics, conceptual formulations (i.e., theology), and ritual all arise out of originating experiences of a Sacred Power, then it is difficult to demonstrate a unity of those founding experiences, let alone their authors. It is not possible, then, to compare whatever Sacred Realities, if any, lie behind those experiences.

Since myths, rituals, ethics, and religious reflection (constructs) all are to be found primarily in the province of social (and institutional) religion, examples of religious socialization and institutionalization will be given in the subsequent chapters, which deal with these separate phenomena. The brief examples that follow illustrate the broader basis of socialization, especially with regard to religious language and terminology. These examples should provide an awareness of the extent to which all religions depend upon socially acquired language structures. Conversely, these examples should reveal the extent to which traditional categories or terms are modified by experiences not fully conditioned by the inherited terminology.

Yahweh as "El"

We have seen already that early Mosaic religion likely received its god's name, Yahweh, from the Midianites through Moses' father-in-law, Jethro. Yahweh was experienced, according to the Exodus account, as an all-powerful deity who was often associated with storms and mountains (i.e., Sinai or Horeb). What may seem surprising, then, is to read in the beginning of the book of Genesis: In the beginning *Elohim* (translated "God") created the heavens and the earth. Upon further investigation many compound names utilizing "El" are used synonymously with Yahweh. For example, in Gen. 14:18-22 we find *El Elyon* ("God Most High"); in Gen. 31:13 and 35:37, *El Bethel* ("God of Bethel"); in five places in Genesis, including 17:1 and 28:3, *El Shaddai* ("God of the Mountain," perhaps "God Almighty"); and in Gen. 16:13, *El Roi* (literally "God of Seeing," perhaps "the God Seen"). Helmut Ringgren assumes that the El-deities were conceived in a variety of ways, since they were attached originally to cultic sites.[27] For instance, *El Elyon* was the high god of Salem (Jerusalem), worshiped by the King of Salem, Melchizedek. Ringgren indicates the strong likelihood that Melchizedek's story derives from David's time (period of the monarchy), at which time *El Elyon* would have been Jerusalem's city-god. The origin and characteristics of a potentially important mountain deity, *El Shaddai* "God of the Mountain"?), are not yet known. Only persons long dead, or evidence yet to be uncovered, would be able to demonstrate any previous relationship of the god Yahweh, who reveals himself on the mountaintop, and the god named *El Shaddai*.

What is important for our consideration is the recognition that the early Hebrews accommodated themselves to their social surroundings as they entered Palestine by incorporating the various names (and some traditions?) of local deities into the traditions surrounding their god, Yahweh. It is known that the Canaanite high god was named "El," also called Father, King, and Bull. He appears in different cultic sites (e.g., *El Elyon* in Jerusalem), usually as a transcendent or otiose deity who was described as the "Highest" *(elyon)*.[28] Beside him stood Baal, primarily a "vegetation" deity who dies and rises, and who was quite popular among the common folk. However, it is not the case that the conceptions and characteristics attributed to El were forced upon, or controlled completely, the nature of Yahweh. Baal, and perhaps El, were sporadically worshiped by Yahweh devotees;[29] still, it is the case that Yahweh's basic attributes arose out of the Exodus events and their interpretation, not from an identification with the Canaanite El. To find Elohim (a plural form of El) as a name used synonymously with Yahweh throughout a complete oral tradition (Elohist) does, however, indicate the great extent to which Yahwism responded to the social and theological situation encountered in Canaan. It would seem that the identification of Yahweh with El may be mostly a case of Yahwist priests seeking to express themselves in terms known and understood in a new and foreign social context. Consequently, many names and concepts are applied to Yahweh, but none control the conception of Yahweh as did the experiences of the Exodus, which gave to Yahweh his supreme position as God almighty in the life of the early Hebrews.

Jesus as Son of Man

As I said previously, the early Christians were for sometime considered a Jewish sect by Jewish orthodoxy. Jesus was born a Jew and died a Jew. Still, with the acceptance of Jesus as the promised Messiah, the early Jewish-Christian sect broke rank with those of the Jewish faith who still awaited the apocalyptic kingdom (e.g., Pharisees and many common folk) and with those Jews who expected no future age or mass resurrection of the dead at all (e.g., Sadducees). The use of the term "Messiah," or "Christ," for Jesus reflects clearly the influence of earlier Jewish eschatological and apocalyptic language and thought upon the early Christian disciples. The term "messiah" itself is not the best example of the influence of apocalyptic speculation on the interpretation of Jesus' life by his disciples. Interestingly enough, it is the simple title "Son of man" that indicates clearly a socially conditioned interpretation of the man Jesus.

In Jewish apocalyptic literature (especially I Enoch) the Son of man is a righteous judge whose coming on earth will signal the beginning of the future (eschatological) kingdom of God's rule.[30] As a preexistent, righteous savior, the Son of man will come to save the righteous and destroy all those sinners who do not worship God. Therefore, he has been appointed as the judge of all people and will sit on the "throne of Glory" and bring all the righteous to him when God's kingdom and reign commences. In IV Ezra, there is a similar figure simply called a "Man" who comes down on a cloud to destroy with fire all evil forces of the sinful age (our world).[31]

The Man spoken of in IV Ezra appears to be the very same Messiah talked about in I Enoch as Son of man. At least this identification seems to be made in the full interpretation (Dan. 7:15-28) that Daniel gives of his vision (Dan. 7:1-14) when he identifies the Son of man as one who comes on the clouds of heaven, as did IV Ezra's man. In fact, the vision of Daniel bears many likenesses to the story in IV Ezra, where the Son of man destroys worldly kingdoms to set up God's rule. Whatever that relationship might be, it is clear that the Son of man is a Messiah-figure who will usher in the heavenly kingdom and judge all sinners. When he comes, he will be righteousness personified and will search out to save only those faithful to God.

Although the duality of earth and heaven, darkness and light, evil and good, present and future age is not described in the fiery detail of the Apocalyptic writers, the early Christian writers use such categories to explain the life and message of Jesus (e.g., John 1:1-18). Furthermore, the use of the term Son of man, for Jesus, indicates a familiarity with apocalyptic language and notions that cannot be denied. Jesus is called Son of man more than seventy times in the New Testament writings, and most often this title is used to refer to the future or eschatological age. For example, the Son of man is pictured coming on clouds accompanied by the angels of God (Matt. 25:31; compare Luke 21:27). Likewise, his task is to destroy sinners (Matt. 13:41) and to be a light in the world—i.e., knowledge and righteousness (Matt. 24:27). Furthermore, this Son of man sits on a heavenly throne (Matt. 25:31 and Act 7:56). Such texts that call Jesus the Son of man parallel too closely I Enoch's Son of man and IV Ezra's Man to allow an independent use of this concept by Jesus' disciples. Consequently, their dependence on apocalyptic imagery is evidence of the New Testament writers' socialization into the intellectual milieu of first-century Palestine. However, it would be a mistake to assume that the social influence of Jewish apocalyptic or any other cultural "reality" is absolutely controlling, as we saw in the case of the Canaanite El.

It appears that the early disciples adopted the late apocalyptic writers' association of the Son of man with the messianic person (as opposed to the whole nation Israel) (En. 48:2b; IV Ezra 8). Therefore, Jesus is quoted as calling himself the Son of man (e.g., Matt. 16:13) and then is identified immediately as the expected Messiah (Matt. 16:16).[32] It is also true that Jesus as the Son of man is expected to usher in God's heavenly kingdom (e.g., Mark 8:38). Furthermore, the author of the Gospel of John has Jesus proclaim himself not only Son of man (12:23) but also the light sent into the world of darkness (12:46). But there are rather dramatic alterations to these seemingly wholesale adoptions of apocalyptic concepts and images when the passage that proclaims Jesus as the light of the world says: "And if any one hears my sayings and does not keep them, I do not judge him; for I did not come to judge the world but to save the world" (12:47).

We are told in the same Gospel only a few chapters earlier that the Son of man has been empowered by God to judge all men (John 5:27),[33] and now a modification of that position is made to bring apocalyptic notions of the judging Son of man into line with early Christian assertions regarding the man Jesus. While the influence of earlier thinkers is faithfully received (John 5:27), it is modified by the very character and mission of the man Jesus as perceived by his disciples (12:47). According to his disciples, Jesus comes as the Son of man—not primarily to judge, but to save. The emphasis of the borrowed concept is clearly altered. Furthermore, the alteration continues with respect to the mission of the Son of man when it is stated: "The Son of man came to seek and to save the lost" (Luke 19:10). The apocalyptic Son of man comes only for the sake of the righteous and does come to judge (cf. John 12:47) the sinners. Yet the Son of man identified with Jesus forgives sins (Matt. 9:6 and Luke 5:24) and seeks to save those who are described as sinners (Luke 19:10).

While there can be no doubt that the early Christians interpreted their experience of the man Jesus in terms and concepts given them by one or another current cultural reality (in this case, Jewish apocalyptic), it is also true that their experience of the man Jesus was not simply controlled or conditioned by these influences. As we shall see in later examples from early Christianity, the experience of the man Jesus had a particular character and impact that could never be fully captured or expressed in the images afoot in first-century Palestine. Gunther Bornkamm, in the context of indicating the familiar apocalyptic terms used by Jesus to proclaim his message, says, "No customary or current conception, no title or office which Jewish tradition and expectations held in readiness, serves to authenticate his mission."[34]

Buddhist Saṅgha

In the Hebrew and Christian examples, I have dealt with some of the social dimensions of language. In this example taken from Buddhism, I want to exemplify briefly the linguistic heritage *and* the institutional nature of the *saṅgha,* or Buddhist "assembly" of monks.[35] *Saṅgha* is a Saṅskṛit term that was, in Buddha's day, used synonymously with *gaṇa* to indicate political, professional, or commercial groups.[36] Many tribal states (like the Licchavis, Vajjis, and Śākhya) prior to Buddha's day were governed by an assembly of elders known as a *saṅgha.* As quasi-democratic states (the elders were not elected by the people they represented), the republics themselves were called *saṅghas* because of their striking form of decision-making.[37] S. Dutt characterizes the *saṅghas,* or republics, this way: "The *Ganas* and *Sanghas* knew nothing of personal rule; they deliberated and acted together, were 'communistic' in their property relationships, republican in the conduct of their affairs and had the tribal council as their organ of Government."[38]

The republican form of government was receding in

Buddha's day partly because of the rise and success of the great monarchies like those of Magadha and Kośala. The republic* in which Buddha was born (Śākhya), for example, was a protectorate of the Kośalan monarchy. In Buddha's era, therefore, the term *sangha* was commonly used to connote the various *śramaṇa* groups, whose ascetics roamed the Madhyadeśa countrysides.[39] These mendicant groups were organized around a teacher and took upon themselves the rules *(vinaya)* prescribed by their leader.[40] Consequently, it can be said that Buddha's assembly of monks *(bhikṣu-sangha)* appears to have adopted its name and pattern from its political, religious, and linguistic environment. As we saw in earlier examples, however, social influence does not mean social determination and control. The Buddhist *sangha* was more than just another *śramaṇa* group.

The most striking difference of Buddha's assembly, often called the *bhikṣu-sangha,* was Buddha's insistence that ideally no religious leader or spiritual teacher, including himself, was needed. In the famous Mahāparinibbāna Sutta ("Sayings of the Final Liberation"—of the Buddha) three related points are made about the nature of spiritual leadership. First of all, the Buddha denies that he is the *śāstri,* or spiritual leader, of the *bhikṣu-sangha.* He says:

> The Tathagatha [Buddha] has no such ideas as that it is he who should lead the community of bhikkhus [*bhikṣu-sangha*], or that the community depends upon him. So what instructions should he have to give respecting the community of bhikkhus?[41]

Second, Buddha insists that the rules of the order *(dharma-vinaya),* not a person, should be a guide after his death.[42] Third, the Buddha is then quoted as saying that each person should be his or her own guide holding fast only to the truth: "Therefore, Ānanda, be ye an island unto yourselves, a refuge unto yourselves, seeking no external refuge; with the Teaching [dharma] as your island, the Teaching as your refuge, seeking no other refuge."[43]

In contrast, the contemporary leader of the Jains, Mahavira, saw himself as the last in a long line of spiritual leaders called tīrthaṇkaras. Buddha rejected the model of disciplic succession and, it appears, utilized his saṅgha for encouraging the practice of the dharma and meditation, while stopping short of forming a cult built around his own authority. This is not to say that the Buddha was not recognized as the central spiritual authority of the bhikṣu-saṅgha, since both laymen and monks extolled the Buddha in the famous three refuges:

> I take refuge in the Buddha
> I take refuge in the Dhamma
> I take refuge in the Saṅgha.

However, one outcome of the Buddha's ideal of self-reliance was his refusal to name his successor, and the saṅghas today still have only institutional heads. A second result of Buddha's insistence on self-reliance is reflected in the operational decision-making of the saṅgha.

Buddha's saṅgha differed not only from the contemporary, teacher-centered śramaṇa groups, but also from the political assemblies in its practice of permitting minority opinions to disrupt the unanimity usually demanded in the political context.[44] Many contending Buddhist sects arose alleging adherence to the command to use self-discovered truth as a guide. Nonetheless, a nonindividualistic goal was encouraged for members of the saṅgha also. One of the phrases used to describe Buddha's assembly was the "saṅgha of four quarters." This phrase indicated the *saṅgha's* spiritual ideal of unanimity and confraternity among its *bhikṣus*.[45] It would appear that the tension between following a common set of rules laid down by the Buddha, and following the dictates of one's own understanding of what is true, resulted in conflicting *saṅgha* aims of desiring unanimity and yet permitting dissent. The *bhikṣu-saṅgha's* ideal included communistic sharing to the extent that the food from one's begging bowl was to be shared with the whole *saṅgha* of monks if necessary.[46] Yet dissenting views among the *bhikṣus* necessitated the ajudication of three different Buddhist councils according to the Pāli Canon. Consequently, the point remains that the Buddha's *saṅgha* cannot be divorced from its linguistic and social antecedents (political and religious), but neither is it fully controlled by them. As N. Dutt remarks, "In Buddhism, therefore, Saṅgha became almost a technical term and was given the same importance as the *Buddha* and *Dharma*."[47]

This remark by N. Dutt points to the development of the *saṅgha* from a mendicant, eremitic group to a settled, institutionalized community. During the early days of the wandering *saṅgha* only the Buddha could ordain a new monk. The aspirant sought entrance with these words: "May we obtain departure from the household life and full ordination from the Blessed Buddha." The Buddha would then respond, "Come, O monk, the dhamma has been well taught, practice the religious life that will make a complete end to suffering." With those words, full ordination was accomplished.[48] As the *saṅgha* developed and gained adherents, it became impossible for all the *bhikṣus* to travel together, and ordination had to be delegated to others besides the Buddha. The only rules imposed on *saṅgha*-ordination were that ten fully ordained monks had to be present and that one of those monks must have received his ordination three years previously. Ordination evolved such that a person was first initiated into the "houseless state" (Pāli: *pabbajja*) as a *śramaṇera* and, usually after the twentieth birthday, into full ordination (Pāli: *upasampada*) as a *bhikṣu*. To enter the homeless state, the initiate simply repeated three times the triple refuge, "I take refuge in the Buddha, I take refuge in the dhamma, I take refuge in the saṅgha."[49] What it meant to take refuge in the *saṅgha* can be inferred from the *śramaṇera's* life, which required ten years of spiritual tutelage during which time the teachings of the Buddha (including the *vinaya* or monastic rules of conduct) were imparted.

Kenneth Chen says that the *saṅgha* was established "in order to provide a favorable climate for the actual pursuit of the path prescribed by the master."[50] The master's path contained over two hundred twenty seven rules (according to the Pāli Canon) as the core teachings of communal discipline called the *pātimokkha* (Pāli term meaning "that which binds together").[51] There were many dharmic responsibilities to learn. But so too was there much spiritual awareness to achieve through moral and meditative activities. One relatively early text declares the aim of *saṅgha* life with the admonition to "go forth and wander about for the good of the Many (Bahujana), the happiness of the Many—in compassion for the world—for the good, the welfare and the happiness of gods and men."[52] Therefore, the *bhikṣu's* primary purpose was to advance on the path to self-realization, but a facilitating requirement and activity was to aid the spiritual development of laypersons who could not devote full time to the Buddha's faith. Reciprocally, laypersons provided daily sustenance, occasional gifts of land, and other such material needs of the *bhikṣu-saṅgha*.[53]

The lofty ideals and rules of conduct of the *saṅgha* translate into institutional control of behavior according to my earlier analysis of the function of religious institutions. The Buddhist *saṅgha* provides one good example of the increasing habitualization of behavior that parallels the establishment of formal social and material institutions. As the *saṅgha* developed from a loosely knit mendicant group *(śramaṇas)* to an occasionally settled rain-retreat community *(āvāsa)* to an established monastery cut off from the eremitic life *(layana)*, social control of thought and behavior increased.[54] As new problems developed in the settled life (e.g., what should be the relationship between nuns and monks who now lived in close proximity to each other for years on end?), rules were created to deal with them (e.g., monks should control the nuns' order, yet stay clear of the temptations women represent).

The *saṅgha*, therefore, represents one example of the impact that language and social institutions can have upon an emerging religious tradition. Not only are the name and structure of the Buddhist *saṅgha* dependent, to a great extent, upon religious and political antecedents, but also, functionally, the *saṅgha* acted to regulate and direct personal and corporate behavior. Furthermore, as the guardian of tradition, the Buddhist *saṅghas* had held three councils by the middle of the third century B.C. to collect, protect, and canonize the teachings of the Buddha.[55] What had begun as an assembly of eremitic mendicants had become an institutionalized order of settled monks.

Summary Comment

One early, interwoven connection of religious experience and social process is to be found in the cultural symbolization system called language. The adoption of culturally available terms and conceptions led the Hebrews to use the borrowed names El and Yahweh for their god. Likewise, the Christian god-incarnate, Jesus, was called the Son of man, a term taken from another religious tradition of the ancient Near East. In the very reception of a religious experience, therefore, language plays a role in shaping conceptualizations and expressions of that experience. Thus, social products (language) and processes (religious instruction) are very early attached to personal experiences of a Sacred. Nevertheless, the powers of language and social process are not conclusive. Both the Hebrew and Christian examples evidence modifications and reinterpretations of the borrowed names. Even when the conceptions were adopted from antecedent cultural systems, the guiding force of interpretation was the experience of the Sacred Power that was being identified.

Habitualization or institutionalization is the second social process that affects the form and character of a fledgling religious movement. For example, the monks who followed the Buddha in the mendicant life-style slowly adopted settled practices that culminated in permanent monastic communities. What had begun as a wandering community of monks in which persons sought the freeing experience the Buddha reported, resulted in monastic schools that debated doctrines, added to the rules of their orders, and regularized their relationships with laypersons who lived in settlements nearby to the monasteries. It is often the case that religious institutions that represent communities and conceptual systems quite different from those of their founders are primarily socially constructed realities. Persons reared in such socially constructed communities may themselves come to accept the beliefs and dogmas of their religion through socialization processes. For such persons, their sacred awareness is better described as a *belief* in the Sacred, rather than a *sense* of Sacred Power.

An example of social religiosity would be the life of a

Buddhist novice or monk who was raised as a Buddhist, schooled as a Buddhist, and lived the life of a Buddhist monk without having had any personal experience (Nirvāṇic or otherwise) that would codify his or her socially acquired religion. The *saṅgha* may control behavior and preserve traditions associated with the Buddha and later followers as one example of the power of institutional control and determination of the religious reality lived in by adherents. Yet, religious institutions preserve and protect the very rituals and myths that can provide, for later generations, codifying religious experiences that make personal a religion socially acquired. We shall now consider examples of those core myths and rituals which bear such a heavy responsibility.

Chapter 3
Myth and Ritual: Expression and Habitualization

Thesis

The basic contention in this chapter is that particular (i.e., core or formative) myths and rituals arise in each religious tradition out of the central religious experience(s) of the founder or founding group as a means of expressing and recreating that founding experience.[1] Put differently, as the genesis of a personal religious movement, the core religious experience serves as an impetus to expression (myth) and activity (ritual), which later become routinized and finally institutionalized. Myth and ritual, therefore, are of the realms of personal *and* social religion, and any inquiry that focuses on one aspect of these phenomena to the exclusion of the other captures only half their potential significance. Furthermore, while some analysts discuss myth and ritual together to establish a dependence of one upon the other (e.g., the myth-ritual theories of Lord Raglan or Robert Graves),[2] the following treatment of them together grows out of a recognition of their interdependent relationship in one specific instance (i.e., core myths and core rituals).[3]

Symbol and Myth[4]

Claude Levi-Strauss, a French anthropologist, reports a ritual incantation of the Cuna tribe of Panama that provides excellent material for a discussion of the nature and function of symbols.[5] The ritual song is called *Muu Igala* ("Muu's Way") and consists of a long incantation that, together with ritual acts of a shaman (medicine—holy man), is intended to facilitate a difficult childbirth. The primary characters of this ritual drama are Muu Puklip, the guardian spirit of babies' souls; the shaman or medicine-priest, called a *nele*; the midwife; singers who surround the pregnant woman; and the pregnant woman.

Both Muu and the *nele* have armies that battle in the climax of the rite, but the assumption is not that Muu is evil, but that she simply has overstepped her bounds as protector of the baby's "soul" and needs to be brought back into line. The various sections of the incantation are repeated as many times as the patient's condition and progress toward delivery require. The woman who lies in distress repeats the words as a participant in, not a spectator of, the ritual. The incantation itself tells the story:

[Condition of the woman: sung by singers *and* woman]
The (sick) woman lies in the hammock in front of you.
Her white tissue lies in her lap, her white tissue moves softly.
The (sick) woman's body lies weak. . . .
Her exudations drip down below the hammock all like blood, all red.
The inner white tissue extends to the bosom of the earth
Into the middle of the woman's white tissue a human being descends.[6]

[Midwife and patient]
The (sick) woman speaks to the midwife: "I am indeed being dressed in the hot garment of the disease."
The midwife answers her (sick woman): "You are indeed

being dressed in the hot garment of the disease. . . ."
The midwife turns about in the hut,
The midwife looks for some beads.
The midwife turns about (in order to leave).
The midwife puts one foot in front of the other.
The midwife touches the ground with her foot.
The midwife puts her other foot forward.
The midwife pushes open the door of her hut; the door of her
hut creaks.
The midwife goes out. . . .[7]

The midwife goes to bring back the *nele,* who upon
entering the hut prepares for the central portion of the rite.
He lights incense of coconuts, and carves small wooden
pieces that symbolize his army *(nelegan).* The army is
described in careful detail as "flat and low, all like bits."
Only such a terrifying army can bring back the captured
soul *(purba).*[8]

[Description of the journey]
The *nelegan* set out, the *nelegan* march in a single file along
Muu's road [i.e., birth canal], as far as the Low Mountain,
The *nelegan* set out, etc., as far as the Short Mountain,
The *nelegan* set out, etc., as far as the Long Mountain, . . .
The *nelegan,* etc., into the center of the Flat Mountain.[9]

On and on goes the description of the "terrain," and then
a technicolor description of a gory battle between the
nelegan and the *muugan* (army of Muu) is given. In the
end, Muu is defeated and the *nelegan* return with the
freed baby's soul *(purba)*—and a baby is born. The
enigmatic character of Muu is indicated when, upon
defeat, she says, "Friend *nele,* when do you think to visit
me again?"[10] Such an amicable response is hardly
expected of a foe beaten in a raging battle.
    The purpose in describing the Muu ritual here is to
demonstrate the various qualities of symbol present in
that incantation. In the first place, symbols have a shared

signification or a cognitive content. Because all symbols are multivocal, they have more than one level of meaning (e.g., womb as birth canal and as fertility of whole earth).[11] Symbols are words, objects, or actions that point to something beyond the everyday connotation of those words, objects, or actions. For example, a common eating bowl, in a Buddhist culture, can symbolize a mendicant's rejection of the world and search for *Nirvāṇa*. Likewise, though in a secular context, a peace sign, written or gestured, signified for many American youth of the 1960s not only peace in Vietnam (explicit meaning) but also shared brotherhood and sisterhood (implicit meaning). Consequently, the *nelegan* are not simply bits of wood, or an invisible army, but the very generative and healing powers of the shaman. A symbol, therefore, points to a reality not easily seen or described. Paul Ricoeur, in describing this characteristic of symbols, calls them "opaque glimpses" of Reality. He concludes, "The symbol yields its meaning in enigma and not through translation."[12] Symbols, therefore, suggest rather than tell, and point toward rather than grasp onto.

The content of symbols must be "shared" in order for them to have meaning for the social group or subgroup that uses them. For example, only when the singers, midwife, *nele*, and pregnant woman all understand the symbols used can the *Muu Igala* ever expect to be effectual. If shared support were lost or the content sufficiently blurred, the symbols of the *Muu Igala* would cease to be ciphers of Muu's reality and thereby would become ineffectual. Symbols are socially dependent in that they usually are chosen from the available language or artifacts of their users' culture. Furthermore, most symbols are restricted in their religious use by their everyday use. For example, the qualities of a deity symbolized by a lightning bolt (e.g., power of a god like

Zeus) would be hard to duplicate with a symbol from a milder context, such as a plough. A symbol's cognitive meaning may provide only an opaque glimpse of the Sacred Reality; yet its referent and nuances of meaning, literal and unspoken, are shared by those who claim the same devotion. This implies that for a symbol to function effectively, that to which it refers (the Sacred) must be known experientially. In other words, not only is the content of a symbol shared but so too is a *sense* of its referent.

In the second place, symbols have not only shared cognitive meanings, but also emotional significance and value. Symbols do not simply convey intellectual understanding, they also engender an emotional response. Seeing a black person raise a clenched fist not only evokes a mental reference to black solidarity or unity, but also shocks the senses (positively or negatively). The vulgar extension of one's middle finger, if done in a certain context, can lead to a very affective response! For many Muslims, the crescent and star evoke a similarly deep emotion. Certainly the Christian cross has had this effect on many believers. There is no doubt the *nelegan* and Muu have this emotive power as symbols when the Muu ritual does accomplish a healthy birth. For a symbol to evoke again and again an unspoken reality or truth, it must speak to a person cognitively and emotionally. When symbols cease to evoke any emotional response whatever, they are no longer capable of providing a sense of self-transcendence. This is often the fate of religious symbols used in creeds or dogmas.

In the third place, religious symbols are integrative and transforming agents. They attempt to point to realities that have been experienced but are hidden from direct vision. As flexible and nondiscursive bits of "language," they quite often arise in attempts to relate religious experi-

89

ences. Because they are multivalent in terms of meaning, they can summarize affective experiences and still integrate such events into the web of everyday sensibilities. For example, to some persons the multidimensional use of the peace sign acts as an organizing influence for all of life. For others, the Wheel of Dharma or the Star of David serves this integrative and transforming function. The symbols of the *Muu Igala* clearly point to the ability of symbols to integrate several levels of human life (rational and emotional) and to transport persons experientially to the realm of the Sacred Power. Therefore, the psychoanalytic interpretation that Levi-Strauss gives, supports the view that symbols have cognitive and emotional content and the power of experiential transformation. The point to be stressed is that without prior validating experiences of the *nele's* power, it would be difficult to evoke the desired psychological response. Symbols can serve religious experience as a profane shorthand. For example, the womb, wood bits, interior "mountains," etc., all are part of the everyday world; but each also points to a facet of the Sacred's domain. When a symbol is received with cognitive and emotional significance, it can transport the devotee out of one mode of awareness and into another. An opaque glimpse of the Sacred becomes a momentary vision.

The journey from symbol to myth is a short one for Paul Ricoeur: "I take myth to be a species of symbol, a symbol developed into narrative form." [13] Ricoeur's definition of myth points to two essential features of myths—their narrative quality and their sharing of the three characteristics of symbols (i.e., cognitive content, emotional significance, and transformational power).[14] While myths may contain elements or symbols that can be viewed synchronically or segmentally in various relationships,[15] it is the diachronic or narrative quality of myths that places mythic events and symbols in a sequential and therefore meaningful order.[16] Thus, in a narrative there *is* a beginning, there are moments of time to which events are set in relationship, and there is an end. Just as reciting the *Muu Igala* song in a jumbled order would render it ineffectual, so also placing the plagues at the end of the Exodus story in the history of Israel would dramatically alter the historical account and its effect. Therefore, an essential characteristic of myth is its narrative, its story form.

But myth, as I shall use it, is a particular kind of story. A myth tells a story of human encounter and interaction with a Sacred Power or Being(s).[17] Therefore, myths are not histories in any sense discoverable by the secular historian. Myths allege to relate human encounters with a Sacred Power or to tell a story about that Sacred Power. Whether the fantastic (by commonsense standards) story of Krishna's appearance as the transcendent Vishnu with many heads, all containing the brilliance of one thousand suns (Gita XI), or the more plausible story of a band of Hebrew tribes escaping from Egypt with divine help (Exodus 3), mythic narratives remain outside the investigative powers of historical research *in their claim of Sacred intervention.* We can use nonbiblical literature and archaeology to support the fact the Hebrew tribes migrated from Egypt, but that Yahweh's presence and power accomplished this escape and journey is not within the province of secular historians to decide.[18]

Many scholars find in Hebrew and Christian mythology an exception to the general rule of myths. They claim that Hebrew and Christian stories are "historically" based and break with earlier cosmic speculations which lack verifiability.[19] Rudolf Bultmann, for example, distinguishes between secular, or profane, history as *Historie*, and "salvation," or sacred, history as *Geschichte.*[20]

According to Bultmann, profane history is the sequence of events as the secular historian studies them. Sacred history, on the other hand, is the history of God's work in the world and therefore can only be understood from the vantage point of faith.[21] Yet, all claims to historicity do not remove the fundamental nature of salvation history's being a "story of the Sacred." Therefore, the Hebrew Exodus story is just as much myth—in the nonevaluative and functional sense in which I use the term—as the Hindu stories surrounding the miraculous biography of the cowherd deity Krishna. It is just that the Exodus story *seems* less problematic, given Western cultures' plausibility structures (*i.e.*, the linear historical view as opposed to the Indian cyclic time scheme). Consequently, *all* myths must necessarily seem fantastic by the standards of other social realities because the introduction of a Sacred, other-world Reality immediately removes myths from the sphere—if not from the criticism—of other social realities. Furthermore, myths vary in types and circumstances, and thus their plausibility among skeptics is weighed differently.

Myths, as stories of Sacred Power or Beings, fall into two basic categories: expressive and reflective. Expressive myths are those sacred narratives which attempt to relate the founding or codifying religious experience(s) of a religious tradition. Reflective myths, on the other hand, are sacred stories composed subsequent to the expressive experience(s) and that attempt, in reflection, to integrate the experienced Sacred into the everyday world. The later, reflective myths explain, defend, and reveal the implications of the Sacred that has previously been experienced. Examples of reflective myths include creation stories, narratives that explain suffering, and sacred or miraculous birth tales. To the extent that reflective myths are separated in time and personal experience from founding or codifying experiences, they do not hold the same status (emotionally or structurally) as expressive myths.

Expressive myths are the ones most central to personal religiosity. When a person has an experience that, for him or her, can only be described as an encounter with a Sacred, that person tries to express in available language and concepts what he or she experienced. Most often that expression or account will use symbols and symbolic language in a story or narrative that attempts to relate in profane terms a reality experienced to be not of the profane world. It is in this process that expressive myths are born. It is true that the expression of the religious experience itself is an interpretation because the language of myth is already socially conditioned. Therefore, the raw experience is never fully known. Yet neither are religious experiences, nor the myths that express them, fully bound by social process or language. The potential for social or cultural breakthroughs always exists.

It should be apparent that myths share the basic features of their relative, the symbol.[22] Myths have a shared intellectual or cognitive content that conveys meaning (both explicit and implicit) to those who value them. The content is the "history" of personal contact with the sacred. Because these sacred stories, or expressive myths, arise from personal experience they are valued as being especially true and as pointing to that which is ultimately real. In other words, these sacred histories have cognitive value. Furthermore, those which arise from religious experience are charged, at least initially, with emotional content. For example, those who say "Jesus died for me" in referring to the Easter story are not making a simple, dispassionate statement. Furthermore, the integrative or transformative ability of symbols may be magnified in myths because of their narrative form. In the telling and hearing of myths the participants are taken back via a

93

story of many parts to the time and place of sacred encounter. Such stories, therefore, provide an existential journey for those who sense a Sacred Power anew in the midst of the mythic narrative.[23] Consequently, the primary transformational quality of myths is their potential for re-presenting or re-creating the original experience they narrate. One should not make too much of this potential in speaking of myths alone, for it is often in conjunction with ritual that myths are used by religious institutions as experiential "transformers."

A final aspect of myths is their exemplary function. Many myths serve as paradigms for behavior. Religious persons attempt to act as their stories of the Sacred indicate they should act. Likewise, the behavior of a sacred or holy person (e.g., a Muhammad or a Jesus) becomes a model for the behavior of later generations. The reason is obvious: the aura of sacredness that surrounds mythic events and behavior imputes to them the value of ultimate truthfulness. Conversely, the careful observer may find in such sacred norms obvious reflections of societal behavior and norms. Ritual behavior is quite often understood as an expressive demonstration of social values and norms.[24] Yet even adopted social norms are modified or molded by the affective dimensions of the religious experience that a core myth relates and a core ritual attempts to re-create.

As in the case of myth, the following discussion of ritual is confined to one primary type—namely, core ritual. Core rituals are those which are associated with the formative or core religious experience and therefore with its myth. In other words, core rituals are those which follow from foundation myths as their active component.[25] To the extent that these rituals represent institutionalized behavior, they belong to the sphere of social religion; but to the extent that they *effectively* re-create (in conjuction with myth) the core experience of a faith, they are of the province of personal religion. The transformational function of expressive myths is shared by rituals that attempt to re-present in a spatial and physical context the core experience of a religious tradition. One clear example of a core myth is the Christian narrative that relates the last meal of Jesus as a sacramental event (e.g., Mark 14:12-26). With the words of institution placed in the mouth of Jesus as the indicator of divine presence, a common meal was looked back upon as an experience of fellowship with the Christian God himself. The early Christian love feast, which later became the ritual called the Eucharist, or Lord's Supper, therefore seems an obvious case of an active, ritual extension of the core myth, which tells of the experiential self-transcendence of the disciples in the upper room.

It appears to be the case that each religious tradition attempts to preserve in its core myths and rituals the experiential power of the genesis experience(s) of that tradition. Many other rituals arise in the institutional context as an attempt to sacralize the lives or moments in the lives of devotees (e.g., ordination and marriage rituals), but these rituals do not bear the same weight of responsibility of codifying for descendants not in memory-range of the core experience the personal religion that necessitated a social form. The core myths and rituals preserved by religious institutions bear the heavy responsibility of re-creating and revivifying personal religion's experience and impulse. Michael Novak comes to a similar, though more general, conclusion when he writes: "Cult is the center of culture. Cult dramatizes the mysterious sources of a culture's vitality. A cult reenacts a culture's sense of reality, story, and symbol." [26] In another place, Novak says, "Rituals and arduous exercises are commonly designed by durable cultures, in order to provide for each new generation an experience of this living recapitulation of the past." [27]

The structure of core rituals provides some clue as to the way in which the "living recapitulation" of past experiences is accomplished. The work of Arnold van Gennep and Victor Turner is helpful here. Van Gennep focused his work on rites of passage (rituals accompanying changes in social position attached to age, social status, etc.). In all such rituals, he found a similar, threefold movement: (1) a *detachment* or *separation* of the participant from his or her position in the social structure, (2) a period of *marginality* or *liminality* in which the participant is suspended between his or her old social state and the new social role that lies beyond the ritual, and (3) a *reintegration* or *reincorporation* back into the social structure (very often with a new and elevated status). [28]

An extended explication of the liminal state is given by Victor Turner, who contrasts liminality, as an anti-structure, experiential state, with structured social relationships. [29] Turner argues that in the midst of a ritual, a state of social and experiential limbo—a betwixt-and-between condition—occurs, in which the participant enjoys social and personal relationships characterized by homogeneity and comradeship called *communitas*. Therefore, communitas is a "modality of social relationship" marked by an egalitarian and humble mood. [30] What rituals provide, therefore, is an "inward experience of existential communitas" (anti-structure), which provides a relief from the everyday world of socially defined relationships (structure). [31]

Turner's analysis seems to provide an answer to the social function of rituals and, as such, to speak to the role of certain rituals within the sphere of social religiosity as I have defined it. For example, the Christian baptismal rituals do separate (confession and purification with prayers), provide a liminal experience (during the humbling immersion in water), and reintegrate (introduction into the membership of the institutional church) the participants. Doctors, garbagemen, nurses—all persons are equal in the midst of the baptismal ritual. In the liminal context of the immersion in, or sprinkling with, water a community of participants is formed that provides a respite from pre-ritual statuses and relationships. Therefore, one function of passage rituals that attempt to provide a new social status is to provide an experience of anti-structure that suspends everyday social structures. Furthermore, the experience of communitas supplies an enduring bond that persists beyond the ritual and that can enrich post-ritual relationships.

There is, however, a second angle of vision that can be used to view the threefold stages of ritual as van Gennep and Turner describe them. The alternative perspective is that of personal religion. Turner states that the modes of structure (socially regulated relationships) and anti-structure (a liminal state of communitas) are not synonymous with secular and sacred distinctions.[32] For example, nonritual statuses and offices have sacred attributes (e.g., divine right of the king) that do not depend upon a constant state of liminality to maintain them. Turner does recognize, however, that such attributes are acquired during rites of passage. What I would call the personal or psychological dimensions of ritual moves beyond the acquisition of sacred designations. The examples that follow seem to demonstrate a homologous, three-phase psychological movement that parallels the three social modalities. In other words, the three modes of separation, liminality, and reintegration may be viewed personally as an exit from profane awareness, personal communication with a Sacred Power, and reentry into the profane mode of existence. For example, the same ritual of

Christian baptism may be experienced as a personal exit from a state of guilt (sin), an experience of forgiveness in a communion with the Sacred Power (*i.e.*, reception of the Holy Spirit), and reentry into the profane world as a "reborn" person.[33]

In the context of personal religion, core rituals may be viewed as the expressive and active re-presentation of the experience related in a core myth of a given religious tradition. This assertion with regard to the major rituals of a religious tradition does not exclude a social interpretation of ritual, but rather qualifies it. Moreover, it should be recognized that there are devotional services (e.g., worship) and expressions (e.g., prayer) that are separate from, yet supportive of, the personal and social goals of core myths and rituals. The twofold perspective of personal and social religion can explain both the habitualization of certain behavior and the ability of that behavior to be self-transcending. Therefore, van Gennep is correct in calling the Christian Eucharist (Lord's Supper) a "rite of incorporation" (into social Christianity).[34] But it is also the case that the same ritual is for many Christians the occasion for renewal of their personal faith. Consequently, it is the dual perspective of personal and social religion that serves best to explain the nature and function of both core myths and the core rituals that attempt to actualize a religious experience even while serving the social needs of the participants. From such a perspective, communitas may be a socially liminal state and/or a state of personal communion with a Sacred Other. Core myths and rituals appear to promote the actualizing of such a twofold awareness of communitas.

Passover as Symbol

The Exodus from Egypt provided the core religious experience for the Hebrew tribes led by Moses. James King

West says: "God's deliverance of the Hebrews from Egyptian bondage is the fundamental premise of Israel's covenant faith and the formulative event without which there would never have been a people Israel."[35] The account of the Exodus relates repeated encounters with Yahweh by the migrating Hebrews and, as the premiere sacred narrative, forms the core myth of early Yahwism. It was in looking at the relationship between the Exodus narrative that recounts Yahweh's acts (*i.e.*, myth) and the yearly Passover sacrifice (*i.e.*, ritual) that I first realized the intimate structural relationship of core myths to their ritual expression. It seemed obvious that the Passover ritual's re-presentation of Yahweh's power and care served essentially as an empirical extension of the Exodus narrative itself. If the story of the Exodus elucidates the commencement of Yahweh's relationship to the Hebrew people, then the Passover ritual attempts to re-create or revivify that relationship.

Besides the familiar Ten Commandments (*e.g.*, Exodus 20), there is in the early traditions a second list of injunctions (*e.g.*, Exodus 34), which was intended to govern the ritual life of the Yahwist community. Scholars have generally referred to the first ten injunctions as the Ethical Decalogue and the second set as the Ritual Decalogue (even though they are actually thirteen in number).[36] On the one hand, the Ethical Decalogue relates the ethical obligations of the Hebrew people with regard to Yahweh, other gods, and one another. The Ritual Decalogue, on the other hand, enjoins particular ritual behavior that betrays a strong cultic influence. The heart of this group of "oughts" is the command for Israel to keep three feasts, or festivals, each year: (1) the Feast of Unleavened Cakes (*i.e.*, the Passover); (2) the Feast of Weeks (*i.e.*, first harvest); and (3) the Feast of Ingathering (Exod. 34:18-26).[37] Exod. 34:18 places first in importance the Passover feast: "The feast of unleavened bread you shall keep. Seven days you shall eat unleavened bread, as I commanded you, at the time appointed in the month of Abib; for in the month Abib you came out from Egypt."[38] In 34:25 the Passover sacrifice is attached directly to the unleavened bread feast. The Passover meal, therefore, is given the special interpretation of being the ritual occasion to commemorate in action what the Exodus story narrates. Let us look at the background of this core ritual and its myth.

The Passover story occupies the place of the tenth plague in the Exodus narrative (Exod. 12:21 ff). According to the story, after the Pharaoh refused time and time again to free the Hebrew people, even in the midst of predicted calamities, the final blow was struck when the angel of death killed all the first-born sons of the families of Egypt while passing over the homes of all Hebrew families. The Passover ritual meal was said to have secured for the Hebrews not only the safety of their first sons but also their collective release from Egypt's grasp. The ritual in Exod. 12:1-20 follows this order: Each family or group of families was to choose an unblemished lamb or kid (goat) on the first day of the seven-day festival and set it aside for the climactic sacrifice at the festival's end. On the fourteenth day of Abib, all the animals were to be killed and their blood placed on the doorposts and door lintels to mark the houses of the children of God. Then the animals were to be roasted and eaten with unleavened bread and bitter herbs. Any part uneaten by morning had to be burned. It is described as a hurried meal eaten with sandals on and walking staff in hand. It was a meal colored by an imminent journey.[39] The ritual described is from the later pen of the Priestly redactors, though its antiquity is attested by the J source (Exod. 12:21-27, 29). In fact, it is likely that the Passover sacrifice was a modification of pre-Exodus clan sacrifices.

Sacrifices were the common mode of worship for the pre-Mosaic clan religions as well as for cults contemporary with Moses in Midian, Canaan, and other places. For example, Jethro (Moses' father-in-law) offered a sacrifice of thanksgiving prior to the Exodus journey (Exod. 18:12).[40] Georg Fohrer sees the Passover ritual as possibly originating from the spring sacrifices that nomadic tribes performed to ensure a bounteous flock or herd.[41] H. H. Rowley agrees, but claims further that the Passover ritual is a Kenite ritual *associated with* Yahweh and was passed from Jethro to Moses as a part of the Yahweh cult.[42] Rowley's analysis would explain why a sacrifice to Yahweh was performed prior to the Exodus journey. Furthermore, a sacrifice by Jethro preceding the flight from Egypt explains why this particular ritual came to be used broadly as symbolic of the whole Exodus event.

One plausible thesis concludes that the ritual described in Exodus 12 actually derives from two rituals: a nomadic animal sacrifice and an agricultural feast of unleavened cakes. This reasoning proceeds: since the Moses tribes were nomadic or seminomadic shepherds with an animal sacrifice, and the Canaanites were settled agriculturalists with a feast of unleavened cakes, the priestly Passover ritual (Exodus 12) represents an amalgam of these two previously separate rituals. This reasoning explains the timing noted in Exodus 12, wherein the Passover festival occurs from the fourteenth to the twenty-first of the month with time for a previous New Year's festival with an animal sacrifice. At least it is known that the Hebrew people celebrated animal sacrifices separate from any use of unleavened bread during their period of seminomadic wanderings.[43]

Whatever the origin of the rite, the Passover ritual was

clearly given new meaning when it was attached to the Exodus story. H. H. Rowley states the principle that "for worship the interpretation is more important than the origin or the form of a rite."[44] Therefore, were we to know fully the history of ancient Near Eastern nomadic sacrifices in general and the Hebrew animal sacrifices in particular, we still would have to grant the ritual new significance and meaning when it is interpreted in light of the Exodus from Egypt. Whatever the original significance of the Passover ritual, "from the time of the Exodus it was forever linked with the memory of the deliverance from Egypt."[45] According to the Exodus narrative, the ancient Passover ritual pointed to the tenth plague in Egypt as an ecstatic experience of Yahweh's active intervention in the lives of the people Israel. Furthermore, the Passover was viewed symbolically as the event that encompassed the *whole* Exodus, not just a single event. The bitter herbs and the unleavened bread symbolized respectively the suffering and servitude in Egypt and the hasty departure. Very early, then, the Exodus events were summarized in a cultic myth of liberation that was celebrated in the Passover ritual of unleavened bread. What was the climactic mythic event of the Passover became a symbol for the whole series of Exodus events, such that the cumulative experience of Yahweh in the Exodus could be re-created with each yearly ritual performance of the Passover meal.

Structurally, the animal sacrifice itself is clearly an attempt at intimate communion with Sacred Power (Yahweh) not unlike such sacrifices in other traditions. At the turn of this century, Henri Hubert and Marcel Mauss, in a classic study called *Sacrifice: Its Nature and Function*,[46] identified three basic stages of animal sacrifices. Using the Vedic Indian and Semitic Passover sacrifices as two illustrative examples, Hubert and Mauss related the three basic stages of sacrifice to be: (1) purification and preparation for sacred encounter (entry); (2) communication with the deity by prayer and through death of an animal (climax); and (3) final purifications to remove any stains of contact with the dead animal and any danger from Sacred Power (exit). The sacrifice, then, can be viewed as a process of sacralization and desacralization that facilitates communication "between the sacred and profane worlds through the mediation of a victim." [47] The purpose of the Passover sacrifice, therefore, is to provide an "intimate communion between the deity and the person sacrificing." [48] Stated differently, for the early Hebrews the animal sacrifice is placed in the context of the Exodus myth as an active attempt to codify that myth experientially for those performing the ritual. In the situation of retelling the Exodus story of Yahweh's might and mercy in the symbols of the Passover narrative (myth), the Passover meal provided the occasion for a renewed relationship of the Hebrew people with Yahweh. This means that the Passover ritual was initially invested with the difficult task of re-creating the experience of Yahweh's power and presence among those who remembered the Exodus journey and, later, among those who lived beyond the founding community.

Baptism and Eucharist as Christ Events

As I pointed out earlier, the early Christian community separated themselves from their Hebrew heritage when they claimed that the Messiah had come in the person of Jesus. As a result, the Hebrew religious traditions were seen in a new light and were given new interpretations. The early Christians claimed an experience of God in the man Jesus, not an experience of Yahweh who had acted in the Exodus on their behalf. Therefore, it was not the Exodus narrative but the stories of the man Jesus as a

103

sacred person (the Messiah) that served as the core myth of the early Christian community.[49] While some Jews saw Jesus as a rabble-rouser or worse, his disciples saw in him God at work (e.g., Matt. 12:22-28). If the Exodus story (*i.e.*, core myth) was enacted in the Passover ritual to evoke renewed awareness of Yahweh's presence in the history of Israel, then the tales of Jesus' words and actions serve a similar function for early Christians who claimed to be baptized in his name and spirit and who attempted to commune with him in the Lord's Supper. These two episodes and their subsequent rituals—baptism and Eucharist—have provided for Christians, throughout the ages, avenues to experiences of God. If it might be said that every occasion of the Lord's Supper, for early Christians, was potentially a communion with the risen Lord Jesus, then the ritual cleansing and confirmation of the baptism was primarily an initiation into that fellowship which communes.[50]

The oldest Gospel account begins its narrative by introducing John the Baptist as one who baptized persons "for the forgiveness of sins" (Mark 1:2-5). His activity was placed in an interpretative framework that ascribed true baptism only to Jesus. He says, "After me comes he who is mightier than I. . . . I have baptized you with water; but he will baptize you with the Holy Spirit" (Mark 1:7-8). With these words the story of Jesus' own baptism by John begins, and Jesus is commissioned by the spirit of God to work out his divine mission (Mark 1:9-11; cf. Matt. 3; Luke 3:1-22; John 1:19-34). In the context of John's baptizing, the act of immersing people in water signified repentance and forgiveness of sins. In the situation of Jesus' own submission to baptism, his act represented for his disciples the commission of Jesus as the Messiah, the chosen one who was to live and to die as God's presence on this earth. Furthermore, for those initiated into the early Christian fellowship, baptism is understood to be the occasion for forgiveness of sins *and* a reception of the Holy Spirit.

According to Jesus' own message, repentance, not baptism, is the initial act in renewing one's life (Mark 1:15). Therefore, the required action of anyone who wanted to enter the early Christian fold was to publicly repent and then to be initiated into the new life by the ritual of baptism. The connection of repentance with baptism of the spirit in the early community is indicated in Acts 2:38, where Peter says, "Repent, and be baptized every one of you in the name of Jesus Christ for the forgiveness of your sins; and you shall receive the gift of the Holy Spirit." So too, the words attributed to John the Baptist by the Gospel writers concur that the baptism that is done in Jesus' name is not simply for repentance and forgiveness, but also for reception of the Holy Spirit (Matt. 3:11 and Mark 1:7-8).

Oscar Cullman says that the early baptismal ritual consisted of two interdependent parts: (1) the act of immersion to cleanse the person from previous sins, and (2) the act of "laying on hands," which transmitted the Holy Spirit.[51] That these two segments of the ritual were separate is not left in doubt by the story in Acts 8:14-24, which tells of Peter and John going to Samaria to transmit the Holy Spirit, "for it had not yet fallen on any of them, but they had only been baptized in the name of the Lord Jesus" (vs. 16).

By the time of John's Gospel traditions, the two functions of repentance and spiritual acquisition had been combined in a baptism of water *and* the spirit. In the story of Nicodemus, for example, the whole image of rebirth in baptism is explained as a personal process and experience (John 3:1-21). Nicodemus is told that unless he is "born anew" he can never enter the kingdom of God. Perplexed,

105

he asks how he can enter his mother's womb a second time. The response of Jesus reflects the early Christian's stress on experience: "Truly, truly, I say to you, unless one is born of water and the Spirit, he cannot enter the kingdom of God" (vs. 5). That is, unless the baptism is one of repentance *and* ecstasy of God's presence, a person will not have entered into relationship with God (*i.e.*, into his "kingdom").

Jesus' own death and claimed resurrection became the analogue for the baptism ritual. New life in the Christian sense requires dying to one's past self-perspective and everyday life and experiencing a new birth of spiritual ecstasy from God's loving presence (*i.e.*, spirit). Consequently, baptism was understood by some early Christians within the context of the concepts of death and resurrection. The apostle Paul states this view directly:

> Do you not know that all of us who have been baptized into Christ Jesus were baptized into his death? We were buried therefore with him by baptism into death, so that as Christ was raised from the dead . . . we too might walk in newness of life. . . . The death he died he died to sin, once for all, but the life he lives he lives to God. So you also must consider yourselves dead to sin and alive to God in Christ Jesus. (Rom. 6:3, 4 and 10, 11)

Cullman notes that this later interpretation markedly affects the expanded function of the rite. First of all, the forgiveness of sins is here based upon the death of Jesus being interpreted redemptively. In the second place, the forgiveness of sins and the reception of the spirit are bound firmly together ideologically. And in the third place, the two functions of forgiveness and reception of the spirit are closely tied to the ritual acts of immersion and emergence from the water.[52] Subsequently, the baptism serves as a rite of passage replete with separation, liminality, and reintegration understood experientially.

The intent of the early Christian baptism was to provide for the initiate an experience in which one rose from the water a "new" person, having died to one's sinful past life. An important point to note is that this ritual was modeled after Jesus' own baptism but interpreted from the perspective of his death and resurrection, *i.e.,* his sacred history.[53]

The story of Jesus' own baptism, therefore, becomes the mythic paradigm, or model, for the early Christians as they went about the process of regularizing and interpreting their ritual of initiation. The baptism was not only a personal experience of repentance, forgiveness, and ecstatic reception of the spirit, but *also* an entrance into the social fellowship of the early Christian community. An early liturgical document, the Didache, says that only those who are baptized may enter into the fellowship of the Lord's Supper.[54] Therefore, baptism potentially provided spiritual experience for a personal faith while at the same time providing entrance into social Christianity and its institutional fellowship. A further example of the centrality of initiatory baptism occurs after the Pentecost experience when Peter admonishes everyone to repent and be baptized in order that the Spirit may be experienced by all (Acts 2:37-39). It appears that the baptism ritual intended for all new Christians to receive as a gift the experience of God's presence (*i.e.,* gift of the Holy Spirit). That the Holy Spirit is linked with the post-death presence of Jesus on earth only further indicates that the baptism experience was meant to be an experience of the presence of Jesus himself. However, since this ritual was usually performed only once, it was left to the Lord's Supper to provide periodic renewal of the experience of communion with Jesus as the Christ.

The second core ritual, the Lord's Supper, was an essential act of worship for the early Christians. The book of Acts tells us that instruction, preaching, prayer, and the breaking of bread were the four primary elements of early Christian worship. It says, "And they devoted themselves to the apostles' teaching and fellowship, to the breaking of bread and the prayers. . . . And day by day, attending temple together and breaking bread in their homes, they partook of food with glad and generous hearts" (Acts 2:42, 46). Cullman says that the ritual reported in I Corinthians 11 and the Gospels is a later interpretation of the Christian community. He shows that the rite described as "the breaking of bread" was part of the regular meal, did not insist upon the use of wine, and was marked by "exuberant joy," *i.e., eucharist.*[55] He continues, "The connection with the blood and in general with the death of Christ seems here to be missing."[56] He further claims that the first meals of the disciples were inspired by the resurrection appearances of Jesus at various and different meals (*e.g.*, Luke 24:30, 36). According to this logic, by placing the breaking of bread in the context of the resurrection appearances of Jesus, the early Christians perceived themselves to be participating already in the messianic meal that commences at the end of this evil age. Yet it is precisely from its development from a common meal context that the Lord's Supper, or Eucharist ritual, appears to go

> back to Jesus' Last Supper before his death. This Last Supper of the historical Jesus is certainly the original source of the community Feast, in so far as it was in remembrance of that Last Supper that the disciples came together after the resurrection to eat the meal at which the risen Christ appeared to them.[57]

One thing is certain: the sacred narratives (myths) that tell of the institution of the Lord's Supper place it in the context of Jesus' final meal (Mark 14, Luke 22, Matthew 26, and I Corinthians 11).

The early Christians are said to have met daily for worship and a communal meal (Acts 2:46 and 5:42, and I Cor. 11:20 and 33). Still, it was not long before the first day of the week (the day of Jesus' resurrection) was set aside as the "Lord's Day" (Rev. 1:10). The celebration of the Lord's Supper continued to be the focus of the worship now conducted weekly (Acts 20:7). Cullman says, "The Lord's Day of the first Christians was therefore a celebration of Christ's resurrection. Each Lord's Day was an Easter Festival."[58] However, there continued at most meetings of the community of early Christians, however frequent, the breaking of bread as a "basis and goal of every gathering."[59] Therefore, in the earliest community, the core ritual was a symbolic meal (or a segment of the meal) where bread was broken and shared as a repetition of the last meal of Jesus with his disciples.

With time, the communal meal developed into an institutionalized sacramental ritual with its primary symbols of bread and wine.[60] The fully developed ritual as found in the Gospels and in Paul's writings focuses upon the fellowship of the participants and their expectation that the Lord Jesus will be present at their table. The "holy kiss" was one sign of this communal spirit ("communitas"? E.g., II Cor. 13:12 or I Thess. 5:26). When such a fellowship was established of those baptized into a "new" life, the expectation was that the same Spirit of Jesus would be present at the ritual table. Cullman puts it this way: "We can see that the whole celebration is directed towards this climax, when Christ comes in the Spirit to his own. . . . Speaking in tongues is perhaps explained as arising from the enthusiasm roused by the experience of Christ's coming in worship in the common meal."[61]

As we saw with the baptism, the Lord's Supper rests

upon an episode in the life of Jesus on earth. Such stories are not simply events in a secular history, however, in that both Jesus' baptism and last communal meal are interpreted in light of the resurrected Christ. Much in the same way that the Passover myth comes to symbolize the whole of the Exodus experience, the Last Supper narrative symbolizes Jesus' life, death, and resurrection. The disciples' fellowship with Jesus is remembered in this event. So, too, does this segment of the Jesus-story serve as a climax to his last, fateful week. Moreover, the Last Supper myth depicts a god-man who will rise from the dead and "drink again in the kingdom" with his disciples. Therefore, this single event symbolizes Jesus' activity and presence—past, present, and future. The attached ritual, therefore, is a "thanksgiving" or "joyous expression" (*i.e.,* Eucharist) of the life, death, and continued presence of the man Jesus. Its primary intention was to re-create the fellowship with the Sacred Spirit or Power that the early disciples had experienced in the life and after the death of the man Jesus. Bread and wine become symbols of body and blood for the purpose of participation in Jesus' continued presence. The baptism is expected to initiate the relational experience that the eucharist repeats.

Regardless of the pre-Christian uses of either ritual, the baptism and Eucharist are interpreted through the life and death of Jesus as central acts of devotion and fellowship with Sacred Power by the early Christians. Inasmuch as they represent routinized behavior, these rituals are segments of the social religion early Christians developed. In the social context, persons could perform or participate in the core rituals with no reception of the spirit or any enthusiasm at all. But only when the participants experienced the presence of the Spirit did the rituals serve the personal religion out of which they grew. Paul says that only those who bare the "fruit of the Spirit" (e.g., love, joy, peace, patience, etc.)—that is, those who live lives altered by Jesus' presence—belong to Christ Jesus and God's kingdom (Gal. 5:22-24). The core ritual of baptism was meant to provide the personal experience of the Spirit that would result in a new life of spiritual "fruits." The core ritual of the Lord's Supper was intended to rekindle the experience of Jesus' presence and to encourage the early Christians in their communal lives to live the gospel of love they preached. E. O. James says succinctly, "In Christian theology the sacraments were instituted to perpetuate the union of God with man in the historic person of Christ as 'the Word made flesh.'"[62]

Buddhist Meditation

Edward Conze, in talking about the primary practices of the Buddhists, says, "In Buddhism the meditational practices are the well from which springs all that is alive in it."[63] Few religious traditions in the world place as great an emphasis on immediate and personal experience of the Sacred Reality and a technique to achieve that experience as do the Buddhists. In the Hebrew and Christian traditions, revelation of the Sacred Power takes place, in the first instance, through historical events and a historical person. In Buddhism, on the other hand, the founder is said to have experienced the Sacred (*Nirvāṇa*) directly and laid out his path for his mendicant followers so that they too could achieve the same immediate experience. The practices enjoined by the Buddha demand far more than meditation alone, as the complex eightfold path indicates.[64] An aspirant must first begin to order his or her ethical conduct *(sīla)* with correct speech, actions, and vocation. Only then can the initiate discipline the mind with appropriate will, alertness, and concentration. The final product of ethical and mental conditioning is wisdom *(prajñā)*, consisting of proper thoughts and understanding of things as they "really are." Yet, in spite of the necessity for ethical preparation,[65] mental discipline is the key to *Nirvāṇa*.

As we saw earlier, Buddha's path was meant to be a map that charted unfamiliar mental terrain. Therefore, in the last analysis, each person is his or her own best spiritual guide. "Be ye lamps unto yourselves," the Buddha says on his deathbed. "Be ye a refuge to yourselves. Betake yourselves not to external refuge. Hold fast to the Truth as a lamp."[66] In the monkish community of the Theravādins, the lonely rhinoceros was the model for the monk who sought the same experience the Buddha had achieved. No intermediary, whether a historical event or a person, can bestow the experience of *Nirvāṇa*. Therefore, in early monastic Buddhism, it was asserted that each person must experience *Nirvāṇa* individually and as the culmination of a long journey involving personal discipline and contemplative effort. Immediate experience alone could sensitize the seeker to the impermanence and suffering that life in *saṃsāra*, the world of repeated births, represents. Only such an experience could awaken in a seeker the awareness of the calm solitude that stands over against the agitated world, like the calm eye in the midst of a hurricane. The provider of that experience is a ritual of mental discipline called "right mindfulness" (Pāli: *sammā-sati*).

The practice of right mindfulness is listed as the seventh step on the eightfold path to enlightenment, although it stands out as the pivotal activity in the quest for enlightenment. Nyanaponika Thera correctly calls the practice of mindfulness the "heart of Buddhist medita-tion."[67] A discourse on proper mindfulness called the Satipaṭṭhāna Sutta occurs twice in the earliest strata of the

Pāli tradition and begins with these words, attributed to Buddha:

> The one and only path, Bhikkhus, leading to the purification of beings, to passing far beyond grief and lamentation, to the dying-out of ill and misery, to the attainment of right method, to the realization of Nirvana, is that Fourfold Setting up of Mindfulness.[68]

Not only was this discourse, which describes techniques to achieve proper mindfulness, a central influence in the early monks' communities, but it continues to be recited in contemporary monasteries and at the bed of dying persons, whose thoughts may be purified merely by the hearing of its powerful verses. The practice of right mindfulness has as its goal a correct appraisal of the total human being, physical and mental, and his or her whole range of experiences. Consequently, attention is focused upon: (1) the body, (2) sensory experiences (feelings), (3) states of mind, and (4) mental contents or ideas. These four areas form the fourfold objects toward which mindfulness is directed.

As we saw earlier, Buddha's spiritual maturation took place in a climate of mendicant asceticism that likely included experimentation with meditation techniques. Apparently, his former teachers Ārāda Kālāma and Udraka Rāmaputra taught the Buddha techniques of mental discipline, although Gautama had judged them to be incomplete.[69] What seems to be clear from the text under consideration (Mahāsatipaṭṭhāna Sutta) is that the early Buddhists' practice of meditation, in its initial stages at least, demonstrates its awareness of Hindu yogic techniques.[70] The famous *sūtra* begins its instruction this way:

> And how, bhikkhus, does a brother so continue to consider the body?

> Herein, O bhikkhus, let a brother, going into the forest, or to the roots of a tree, or to an empty chamber, sit down cross-legged, holding the body erect, and set his mindfulness alert.

> Mindful let him inhale, mindful let him exhale. Whether he inhale a long breath, let him be conscious thereof; or whether he exhale a long breath, let him be conscious thereof.[71]

Unlike classical yoga, the goal of which was to still the mind completely, the Buddhist practice of mindfulness was intended to recondition and to sharpen conscious processes so that the mind would be swept clean of hindrances and made attentive in order to receive intuitive wisdom. Still, the shared meditation techniques included a lonely, peaceful setting, a fixed body posture, and concern with the natural process of breathing. However, while the yogins actually practiced breathing exercises, the Pāli texts enjoin the Buddhists only to observe the breathing process.[72] The similarities between the two systems soon end.

As the first step on the path to an alert mind, awareness of bodily processes was supposed to evoke an experience of detachment from those very processes. To observe one's breathing grounds awareness in detachment so that the practitioner can say, "Conscious of my whole body will I inhale. . . . Conscious of my whole body will I exhale."[73] The same awareness can be focused upon all bodily activities, such as walking, sitting, lying down, with the thought, "There is the body."[74] The goal of these exercises is to sense the transitoriness of the body. Proper mindfulness with regard to bodily parts is the next step of the reflections on the body. In this context, the body is considered as a conglomerate of impurities including "excrement, bile, phlegm, pus, blood, sweat, fat, tears, serum, saliva, mucus, synovic fluid, urine."[75] After one contemplates the primary material composition (earth, water, heat, and air) of the body parts,[76] the Pāli text urges consideration of corpses. From the swollen, blue-black corpses to barren skeletal remains, the *bhikṣu* is urged to recognize in them his own body.[77] The net effect of these contemplations is the realization that "the body is something that comes to be or . . . something that passes away; . . . conscious that 'There is the body,' mindfulness hereof becomes thereby established."[78]

The second stage of mindfulness focuses upon the feelings. Whether painful, pleasant, or indifferent, feelings that arise from sensual contact with the world bind a person to the world. Anger, lust, and boredom all attach a person to the object of those feelings. Again the goal is for the mind to be alert in watching feelings come and go. Just as the body is born and dies, so do feelings rise and fall. The mindful person does not participate in, but rather observes feelings come and go.[79]

The third phase of mindfulness is watching the thoughts of the mind ebb and flow. When thoughts arise as the result of feelings, the alert *bhikṣu* will say, for example, "My thought is lustful . . . or . . . there is a thought" (XXII. 299). Watching the state of mind change from one thought to another is the third stage of alertness.

Ever inward, the fourth plateau of mindfulness is located in alert observation of the ideas, truths, and qualities that hinder or aid enlightenment. The text lists objects for mindful contemplation that hinder (*e.g.*, lustful desires, ill will, hatred) or aid (*e.g.*, equanimity, tranquility) enlightenment. The Four Noble Truths themselves are judged to be beneficial objects of mindful observation.[80]

The practice of the fourfold stages of right mindfulness or attentiveness leads to the four jhñānic or contemplative states, which culminate in wisdom *(prajñā)* and Nirvāṇic calm—*i.e.*, the same experience the Buddha had according to the text. The ritualized practices described in the Satipaṭṭhāna Sutta permit the initiate to know, to shape and, to free the mind through the four stages of mindfulness.[81] The greatest hurdle facing the *bhikśu*, according to this text, is his attachment to his body. Therefore, the lengthiest and most elaborate guidance is given in the section on observing the body and its decay. The cemetery techniques (observation of corpses) may seem grotesque and repulsive to many Westerners (and, in fact, were seldom used), though attentiveness to the cyclic decay of the material world is the primary goal for the monk. It is when the *bhikśu* "knows" through mindful observation that the body is an *anitya* (impermanent) object that the body can be controlled to work for the seeker's enlightenment. The remaining stages of mindful observation focus inward through the feelings, mental states, and resulting ideas a person can hold. In each stage the ideal is to observe the feeling or idea in a detached way. In each stage the mind becomes tranquilized by its being placed in the role of the observer. The Satipaṭṭhāna Sutta ends with the same claim it makes at the beginning—that fourfold mindfulness is the "one and only path" to *Nirvāṇa*.[82]

What the fourfold path of mindfulness intends is a re-creation of the experience the Buddhist tradition attributes to the Buddha.[83] The whole narrative of Buddha's life (his princely state, renunciation, seven years' wandering, and enlightenment experience), as conveyed in oral traditions, would have served as the full myth that grounded the ritual of right mindfulness. But it is the story of Buddha's enlightenment of four stages and three bodies of knowledge that provided the central mythic event that the meditation ritual of right mindfulness intended to reenact. Therefore, not only are the same levels of consciousness reached as the Buddha reached, but the same self-evident truths result in the practice of right mindfulness. At the end of the mindful path awaits an intuitive knowing of *anitya* (impermanence), *duḥkha* (suffering due to attachment), and *anātman* (sense of selflessness).[84] Therefore, what is taught to a novice as the "truths" of Buddhism is experienced as a "true-for-me" subjective knowledge when the goal of mindfulness is attained. The Buddha spoke of joy and calm in connection with his experience of *Nirvāṇa*, but the path he outlined (and others expanded upon) deals with the practical knowledge that can be transmitted through the discipline of mindfulness, not with the enigmatic qualities of *Nirvāṇa*, which could become the objects of debate.[85] Consequently, the narrative of Buddha's encounter with the sacred calm called *Nirvāṇa* (a myth) acts as a paradigm for the mental discipline of mindfulness (the ritual of meditation) assumed by those who followed him. The impetus to meditate, therefore, is given by the story of Buddha's own meditative experience. Drummond agrees when he says of Buddha's experience, "Its importance was such as to make direct or personal experience a primal element in the entire movement that the Buddha initiated."[86] I have gone further to say that the story of Buddha's experience not only gives rise to later attempts to repeat it, but also orders the content of what is subsequently experienced. It is not just any personal experience that is sought in the disciplined practice of mindfulness, but the experience of the impermanence of the visible world *(anitya)*, the sorrowful nature of the life process *(duḥkha)*, and the illusory nature of even a divine self *(anātman)*.

An example of the knowledge achieved by right mindfulness is the story of the Elder *(Thera)* Mahatissa. Once, while gathering alms in the city of Anurādhapura, the *bhikśu* Mahatissa passed by a beautiful woman who had left home after a quarrel with her husband. As the husband sought for his wife he asked Mahatissa if he had seen a beautiful woman traveling on that same road. The monk responded:

> Whether what went along here
> Was a man or a woman, I do not know.
> But a collection of bones is moving
> Now along this main road.[87]

Such is the response of one who has achieved total detachment from *saṃsāra* and has arrived at the end of the road of right mindfulness. Such is the response of one who claims the same intuitive experience and perception the Buddha-myth tells.

Summary Comments

To call the Exodus story or the narrative of the life of Jesus a myth may startle some readers. It may be less difficult for some to accept such a designation of the somewhat cloudy tale of the Buddha's spiritual quest and enlightenment. The reader should recognize that my description of expressive myths includes only those stories which claim the intervention or activity of a Sacred Power *and* which intend to relate and to describe an awareness of that Sacred Reality. Descriptively and functionally, then, all three stories related above (the Exodus, Jesus as risen Christ, and Buddha's enlightenment) are core, expressive myths. The question of the historical foundations of these narratives is muted by their placing of Yahweh, Christ (God), and *Nirvāṇa* at the center of their stories.

The difference between legends and expressive myths is the latter's inclusion of a sacred dimension that controls the interpretation and experiential value of the story. Consequently, an expressive myth is any delineation of an

118

experience with a Sacred Reality that provides a comprehension of that special Power. Furthermore, it is assumed that expressive tales have an experiential and therefore historical basis. Whether the story of a vision, an encounter with a holy man, an accumulative understanding of historical events, or an ecstatic experience of the power of the sun, an expressive myth serves as the founding and core influence in the development of both personal expression and social habitualization.

Rituals attached to the core myths appear to be charged with the difficult task of re-presenting or re-creating the experience of the Sacred the narratives relate. From this perspective, such rituals may be viewed as performances of key mythical passages. The Passover festival culminated in a sacrificial enactment that relived the power and protection of the Yahweh experienced in the Exodus. The Christian baptism and Eucharist ceremonies attempted to enliven in the faithful a sense of the presence of and communion with the man-god Jesus. The fourfold practice of mindfulness (as an early form of Buddhist meditation) attempted to awaken in the devout monk an awareness of the impermanent nature of the self and the material world, as well as provide the occasion for a reception of the sacred calm of Nirvāṇa.

Functionally, the rituals share a similar task. On the level of social process and form, all three rituals evidence the limitations and impositions of social form in the language, symbols, and activities prescribed. On another level, these rituals can be understood to have provided a sense of communitas or anti-structure that sacralized life. What is even more clear, however, is that each of these rituals was structured to make available an experiential transition into the realm of Sacred Power. The threefold movement of rituals described by Turner, therefore, may be regarded from the perspectives of both social process and personal experience.

Obviously, not all myths and rituals serve the function and purposes of core expressions and activities. Hymns, prayers, and public worship all contributed to the personal and social dimensions of Hebrew and early Christian religious awareness. Fortnightly recitations of the sacred canon and public teaching sessions also added to the religious commitment and experience of Buddhist monks. Still, the impetus of personal religious experience and the socialization of those experiences can be observed most directly in the core myths and rituals, which are charged with transporting the devout to confirming encounters with the Sacred Reality—be it Yahweh, Christ, or *Nirvāṇa*.

Chapter 4
From
Imperative to Ethic

Thesis

In this chapter the behavioral "effects" of both personal and social religion will be explored. A distinction will be made between existential imperatives, which arise as the result of religious experience, and ethical pronouncements, which originate primarily from social processes. Because personal religion arises chronologically prior to its social routinization, it follows that the ethics or morals maintained by religious institutions will reflect the basic imperative that arises from the core religious experience. Consequently, religious experiences give impulse not only to symbolic expression (myth) and re-creation (ritual), but also to attitudes and intentions, which are reflected in behavior. Such behavior is a mark of the "reborn" person, whose conduct represents the tangible effects of an immediate core, or codifying, religious experience. To be sure, the religious institution or social religion may add to, or even alter, the demands that are made by the core experience. Likewise, the ethics of a religious institution may reflect the mores of the surrounding culture or society. But implicit, if not explicit, in all decisions to expand or amend ethical codes is the

121

intent to judge any new formulations against the founding or later codifying impulses. Consequently, when these impulses weaken, social religion is guided by traditions that only imperfectly contain the initial imperatives. In sum, a founding, or core, religious experience provides not only core myths and rituals, but also core impulse(s) or imperative(s) that are externalized as the ethical norms of the religious institution. Social factors (language, customs, etc.) play a role in the process of externalization. Consequently, the end result of the process *may be* that the socially derived institutional ethics actually conflict with the core impulses that gave birth to them. Whatever the final result, personal and social religion interact in the area of ethical behavior. This interaction will now be explored.

Imperative to Ethic

R. D. Laing's basic axiom for his psychological theories is: "Behavior is a function of experience; and both experience and behavior are always in relation to someone or something other than the self." [1] Behavior is a key to any analysis of another person's experience and attitudes because what one person experiences is never known experientially to another except by analogy. I cannot experientially know your parents the way you do, nor can I say for certain that my experience of *satori* (Zen enlightenment) is the same as yours. It is when we act spontaneously of one accord again and again that we know that our claim to a shared, experiential impulse has some substance. The power of experience in molding behavior is obvious in the socialization of children. Parents may tell their children time and again of the importance of such cultural or religious values as unselfishness or nonviolence, as they encourage the sharing of toys or discourage the hitting of a playmate. But if those same parents consistently abuse persons of another race, or fight and argue incessantly with each other, it should be no surprise when their children exhibit behavior similar to the parents' actions, rather than heeding their admonitions. Therefore, behavior is one key to understanding the experiences of another person.

William James says behavior is the empirical criterion for assessing the quality or validity of a religious experience. He argues that a religious experience ought to be judged not by its origins, but by "the way it works out on the whole." Appealing to a famous American theologian, Jonathan Edwards, James makes this point in the Christian context:

> There is not one grace of the Spirit of God, of the existence of which, in any professor of religion, Christian practice is not the most decisive evidence. . . . The degree in which our experience is productive of practice shows the degree in which our experience is spiritual and divine.[2]

Our examples will show that religious traditions around the world emphasize an intense interest in behavioral conformity to expressed goals and experiences. It seems to be the case that all religious traditions evidence an interdependent and necessary relationship of conduct to experience. In another context, Huston Smith distinguishes drug experience from religious experience on the basis of resulting behavioral differences. In his essay entitled "Do Drugs Have Religious Import?" he asserts that "drugs can induce experiences that are indistinguishable from religious ones." Then Smith goes on to qualify this claim by saying, "Drugs appear able to induce religious experiences; it is less evident that they can produce religious lives."[3] The two experiences compared earlier (one drug-induced, one not) both seemed to fit the four qualities outlined by James for religious experience.[4]

However, both experiences may not have produced religious lives, and, in Smith's fuller sense, they were not religious. *What we may now say is: behind every religion lies a personal religious experience, but not every experience that appears religious (of whatever origin) necessarily leads to a personal religion.* Only when persistent application of a religious experience ensues, does a personal religion arise. In other words, personal religious experience is not synonymous with personal religion. The latter is more than ecstatic experience, it is a whole mode of living.

That those religious traditions which do endure depend upon formative experience for their code of conduct is an assumption that follows naturally from the above discussion. Especially when the religious experience is immediate or ecstatic does a person feel impelled to act in accordance with the "illumination" received. The current dramatic conversions of the so-called Jesus freaks are good examples of this process. Young people who have been converted usually refrain from behavior deemed acceptable previously, such as the use of drugs and alcohol or engagement in sexual promiscuity. Furthermore, new behavioral rules and habits are adopted. This attention given to behavior is a sign of the impact that religious experience can have on the religious life conceived personally.

The committed life of personal religion, then, is an active extension of religious experience. Consequently, the saint or holy person attempts to act in a *consistently* righteous way. In other words, with religious experience comes an impulse to act according to the character of that experience. Therefore, sustained behavior in accord with the religious impulse indicates that a conversion has taken place.[5] While we cannot know whether or not religious lives did follow from the two experiences cited earlier, we may note that the experience of Person B (not drug related) announced the "foundation principle of the world" to be love.[6] Only if Person B persistently externalized that insight in behavior could we talk of his or her experience spawning a personal religion. As we saw earlier, such a realization led Wack to incorporate altered behavior as a criteron for any experience being called religious.

Furthermore, the motivation to love, in this instance, is a "core impulse" or altered intentionality of the person having the religious experience. Such religious impulses are not captured in lists or systems of ethics, even though those lists or systems may be the objective expression of motivations or imperatives. As we shall see, the externalization process related to behavior is homologous with that of myth-making.

A core religious impulse, therefore, is just that—an impelling, intentional force or impetus that gains objectivity or exemplification in the concrete situations of ethical behavior.[7] For example, the enlightenment experience of an ascetic may result in a sense of detachment from the world that impels the sage to act impersonally toward other persons. Furthermore, a religious experience may bestow a multifaceted impulse that is not reducible to a single descriptive word or phrase (compare Buddha's impulse toward nonattachment and compassion). Intentional complexity is analogous to the difficulty in describing in one word a Sacred Power that is experienced as terrible and tremendous, yet loving (e.g., Yahweh). Whether simple or complex, personal religious experiences usually lead to religious behavior that reflects the impulses granted in those experiences. Because core experiences are received in a variety of cultural and personal contexts, they impart impulses that are just as varied. As a profound influence on the life of a person, a codifying experience may impart a consistency or unity to subsequent behavior that identifies the core impulse. The imperatives of personal religion, therefore, are less a system of ethics than a coherent drive toward a particular type of behavior (e.g., nonviolent or loving).

The personal religions that endure develop social forms of expression (including mythic expression and ritual reenactment) as well as institutionalized norms of behavior that extend from the core experience and its impulse. It is in the routinization process that an impulse becomes a reflective assertion of proper conduct—i.e., an ethical demand. Proper behavior, therefore, may be in the first instance a concern of personal religion, but quickly it is taken up as a segment of the externalizing process. The end result is that what began as expressions of an experiential drive may for later generations be experienced as the ethical commands of the religious institution that states these rules as givens of conduct. Such behavioral norms are to be accepted, internalized, and lived out, whether or not any experiential drive or impulse to enact them exists.

A social religion's behavioral norms are formed primarily by the processes of reason acting upon experiential data. Therefore, what is experienced as an impulse to act in a loving manner can be translated—and transformed—in available language to *rules* or *laws* of love. Institutional lawmakers attempt to relate faithfully the core religious imperative to all behavioral situations. Consequently, as problems or questions arise in the context of living, ethical pronouncements are made that evidence the interaction between personal and social religion. Furthermore, the ethics of social religion are rendered in the language and concepts given in the social context. Likewise, the customs or mores (same Latin root as "morals") of a society will propose behavioral issues and decisions to be considered in light of the core religious experience. Social customs must be confirmed, denied, or modified by resident religious traditions—they cannot be ignored.[8] One result of this interaction is that the ethical pronouncements of social religion and its institution often stray far afield from their original impulse. It would appear that any religious reality—either personally or socially understood—is forced to relate its behavioral norms to all phases of secular experience to gain plausibility with nonadherents as well as with devotees. Whether the religious impulse is to reject all secular norms and experiences as transitory (e.g., Buddha's nonattachment) or to accept all worldly events as instances of a Sacred's activity (e.g., the Hebrews' experience), the fact remains that a religious imperative seeks to transform *all* of life, not just a segment of it.

The far-ranging ethical demands of religious institutions are the products of a dialectical interaction between personal and social religion. However, the ethical commands that attempt to capture the core religious impulse (e.g., love or detachment) are usually granted a premiere place among other social religious norms. Consequently, in some religious traditions, dietary laws may be peripheral (e.g., Christianity) and in others more central (e.g., Buddhism). Furthermore, a basic standard for deciding religious commands or norms is the statements or behavior of the founder(s)—that is, the first externalization of the core impulse. This is especially true for the earliest community. A similar decision-making process occurs personally for those who have codifying experiences that bestow impulses similar to that of the founder. For the realm of social religion, however, there is usually some person or group of persons who by his or her office makes official ethical decisions and pronouncements (e.g., the Pope or a Council of Bishops) whether or not that person has had a personal religious experience.

A person's private religious imperative might lead to behavioral decisions that conflict with that of the religious institution on a particular matter (e.g., the Catholic institution's conclusions regarding birth control). I do not mean to imply that a personal codifying experience necessarily will best reflect a religious tradition's moral imperative, for the value and weight of tradition is that it is the accumulation of many persons' experiences over a period of time. Nonetheless, what is an ethical command to the institution must become an experiential imperative for a person to feel compelled to act in accord with the ethics of that religious tradition. Social situations, including language, often change from the day of the founder to the time of the contemporary devotee, and the original or founding impulse needs to be re-experienced if traditional ethics are to have any application personally.

When social religion in its ethical statements strays too far from its initial impetus, it is in danger of mirroring the society it pretends to sacralize.[9] An essential claim supporting religious ethics is their sacred sanction. The behavior that is demanded as a part of being religious usually confronts the socially integrated person as restrictions or prohibitions of many secular activities. For instance, dietary laws that forbid the use of alcohol or the eating of meat pose such a confrontation. Furthermore, cultural ideals, such as those of material success, are usually attacked by sacred norms that deprecate the ability of a worldly person (e.g., the wealthy) to come to true experience of the Sacred. Therefore, religious ethics—especially in their institutionalized form—may be viewed from the outside as negations of everyday life. But for the person who is moved by the impulse provided by

personal experience, ethics are existential imperatives—
i.e., behavior he or she *wants* to perform and that is
satisfying to perform. While sexual abstinence may
appear restrictive to the secular person, to a devout
Buddhist monk it may provide freedom to pursue his
spiritual quest uninterrupted.

Proper behavior is the concern and the product of both
personal and social religion. What is personal imperative
for the founder(s) or those who have codifying experiences, remains ethical demands for those living within
the sphere of social religion. What one person feels
motivated to do, another person feels forced to do. The
authority in the first instance is the Sacred as experienced;
the authority in the second case is the religious institution
or its designated official. Consequently, without a codifying experience, personal motivation to adhere to an
institution's ethics is lacking. F. Ernest Johnson recognizes these two levels of ethical commitment as he says:

> It would seem useful to bear in mind as one reads that the
> possibility of maintaining ethical sensitiveness without any
> clearly defined religious faith is a simple empirical fact. What
> remains undemonstrated is whether or not, generation after
> generation, a "Puritan conscience" will sustain itself without
> the undergirding of something approximating a Puritan's
> faith.[10]

Johnson says that the danger of arguing for ethics simply
as the sanctions of religion is that ethics are best
understood as a "commitment to a way of life." The ethics
of any religious tradition, therefore, are best discovered by
examining the lives of the "holy men" and "sacred
women" of that tradition, along with any expressed lists
of "oughts." In the examples that follow, an attempt will
be made to recognize both levels of oughts. Furthermore, I
shall try to indicate the traditional importance certain

core imperatives or ethics have had. Throughout, I shall use "imperative" to refer to the central impulses that personally motivate behavior, and "ethics" to indicate institutionally developed and proclaimed religious laws (whether or not these laws have at their root a core experience).

The Covenant Impulse in Yahwism

"Law and order" is not a new slogan to Americans of the mid-twentieth century. Its use, of course, has been subject to the same social and cultural limitations and abuses that any issue or idea endures. What is of benefit to discuss here is the relevance of secular appeals for law and order to the same appeals made in the religious context. Given the current rise in the crime rate and the relative lack of safety in simply walking the streets of our cities and suburbs at night, the call for law and order seems a natural consequence. Less apparent are the factors that, when present, facilitate and encourage adherence to the laws and customs of a society.

There are at least three conditions that contribute to behavior conforming with the laws of society. Obedience to the law may occur: (1) when the laws are viewed to be just and justly administered; (2) when the laws are considered to be permanent and have stood the test of time; and (3) when the authority administering the laws is respected (perhaps even feared) as being powerful enough to ward off any threat to the accepted legal system or as being able to enforce obedience. The first inducement to conformity should be obvious. Laws that are experienced as unjust are ignored or broken with little consideration. When the first women priests were ordained recently in the Episcopal Church, the presiding bishops ignored demands to stop the proceedings because they considered the church's law to be discriminatory and unjust.

Likewise, if a law is administered unjustly it will gain little respect or adherence. Minority groups who feel discrimination in terms of their treatment with respect to enforcement and prosecution under the law have consistently dissociated themselves from that law and its keeping.

The second condition is also fairly obvious. Laws recognized to be permanent carry the weight of time and precedent. When a law is experienced to be temporary, for whatever reason, there is a feeling that it really must not be of as great importance as those which endure. For example, when the Eighteenth Amendment to the United States Constitution, prohibiting the making or selling of alcoholic beverages, was passed, the widespread disregard of it was based, at least in part, on the general feeling that it was an unrealistic law that would not survive the test of time. Perhaps a similar disregard is felt by some for laws related to the use of marijuana in our own day. Certainly, widespread disregard of wage-and-price controls during the Nixon administration could, in part, be attributed to feeling that they were both unjust and transient.

The third factor—powerful authority—is sometimes the only inducement to obey laws for those who have judged those laws to be unjust and/or temporary. Certainly, awareness of government prosecution was a major encouragement for observance during the wage-and-price controls. Or again, for many persons, conformity to Hitler's Nazi rule was largely a matter of submission born of fear. The authority of a Sacred Power, also, can provide a powerful incentive to obey religious laws, as Hebrew religion will show. Consequently, when persons feel included under a system of law (because it is fair *for them*) that is enduring, the presence of a powerful ruler or judge can provide a feeling of security and comfort. Therefore, laws that operate in this threefold context can be expected to be appreciated, not simply endured. Such laws are seen as benevolent protection, not legalistic tyranny. This is the context in which I would place the laws of ancient Israel.

The experience of Moses and the Exodus tribes was of a compassionate, mighty, and jealous God, Yahweh. H. H. Rowley says, "The most significant things that are taught about God's character . . . all spring from Israel's experience of God in the period of the Exodus." [11] Rowley later continues, "In all this he revealed himself as a compassionate God . . . an electing God, a mighty God, and a saving God. Israel's faith was based not on speculation, but on experience." The laws of the early Hebrews, from their perspective, were not simply commandments arising from a group of legalistic lawmakers. Rather, the attitude derived from the Exodus experience was an awestruck gratitude for a mighty god and his demands. Exod. 20:5b, 6 reports, "I the Lord your God am a jealous God, . . . showing steadfast love to . . . those who love me and keep my commandments." The feeling of inclusion under a just and eternal law given by the most mighty of all gods seems to be the experience of many early Yahwists. For them, says Fohrer, their religion was "not a religion of law, but a religion of life according to sanctified rules expressing God's will." [12]

The Sinai story is an expression of the Hebrew's ethical relationship to Yahweh. According to the Sinai tradition, it was on that holy mountain that the covenant between Yahweh and his people was initiated. This bond at first did not include the long list of demands found in the book of Exodus. In fact, it is generally accepted that the Ethical Decalogue (Exod. 20:1-17), which stands at the heart of the Sinai narrative, is itself a collection of laws from a variety of sources. Fohrer explains that decalogues were common throughout the ancient Near East and that the Ethical Decalogue is likely a compilation by the E writer from other sources.[13] Importantly, the material that *both* the Ethical (Exod. 20:1-17) and Ritual (Exod. 34:10-27) Decalogues include refers to the experience of Yahweh's power and authority. In both decalogues three apodictic commandments appear, which demand: (1) that Yahweh alone shall be worshiped (Exod. 20:3 and 34:13-14); (2) that no godly images are to be made (Exod. 20:4-5 and 34:17); and (3) that the Sabbath shall be observed as a day of worship and rest (Exod. 20:8-11 and 34:21). Consequently, the primary impulse of gratitude and trust is evidenced in the imperatives that demand complete obedience to Yahweh and his will. He is the mightiest of all gods and, therefore, exclusively to be worshiped. He transcends the gods of earth, whose idols representing animals or men cannot capture the truth that is Yahweh.[14] The attitude or impulse to praise Yahweh for his mighty acts and compassion is fully regularized in a special day of worship—the Sabbath. In all three of these commands an overriding impulse of gratitude and awe is expressed. The imperative that was meant to guide the life of piety is not any one of these rules of conduct alone, but, rather, a sense of gratitude and awe that would impel a member of the Hebrew community to attempt to live in accord with Yahweh's will. There was little legalism bound up in personal obedience to Yahweh. Rather, as Rowley puts it, "Israel's Covenant was born of gratitude and was freely entered into. God's claim upon Israel was established by his deliverance of her, not by his conquest of her."[15]

Still, to those apostates who lacked personal experience of Yahweh even from Israel's beginning, the covenant's demands would have seemed oppressive. In the earliest community there appears to have been pressure to respond to daily problems of conduct, as well as to the established ethical codes present in the surrounding societies. What should be the proper attitude and behavior with regard to slaves (Exod. 21:2-11) or toward serious, capital crimes (Exod. 21:12-17)? The so-called Covenant Code (Exod. 21:22–23:19), which developed over a long period of time and was appended to the earlier Ethical Covenant, takes up just such everyday matters. Fohrer comments on the apparent random inclusion of ethical issues: "The selection of material treated in these collections appears haphazard at first glance. . . . However, it is probably determined by their intent and purpose."[16] He indicates that not only decalogues but other ethical codes as well (such as the Babylonian Hammurabi Code) were available to the early Hebrew settlers of Canaan. Social influences on the formation of ethical codes are apparent. For example, the Ritual Decalogue likely existed as a ritual code related to the cult of Yahweh among the Kenites or Midianites.[17] In a similar manner, the Covenant Code appears to represent a later (monarchy period) addition of laws, which are "in part the product of a compromise between Yahwism, the remnants of the clan religions, and Canaanite religion."[18] Consequently, the laws of the Torah may be viewed as eclectic borrowings, grouped in a "scissor and paste" fashion, and marked by no guiding organizational thread.

As we saw with the Passover ritual, it is not the origin of a rite, or in this case a group of laws, that necessarily determines its meaning or use for the people borrowing it. Consequently, it would seem that the whole collection of laws (the Torah) that are gathered in the Pentateuch represents a systematic attempt to apply the core impulse of awe and gratitude toward Yahweh to its fullest extent in directing *all* aspects of life.[19] While various ethical codes were available and adopted to various degrees, the relationship of the many laws of the Torah is to be found in their inclusion within the covenant relationship characterized by grateful obedience to the mightiest of all gods, Yahweh. The covenant relationship was a relationship born out of the Exodus experience (especially a mountain event) and thus carried a special meaning for the early Hebrews. Therefore, the institutionalization of personal Yahwism led to a continued attempt to expand the rules of conduct to include all of life. What resulted was a legalization of what had been heretofore a life commitment based upon the covenant experience with Yahweh. Fohrer refers to this development as a move from the Mosaic regulations "to a goal Moses can hardly have had in mind: a comprehensive system of commandments and prohibitions regulating the entire life of the nation and the individual, such as the Jewish religion of the law envisions."[20]

The difference between existential imperative and institutional law is the difference between a deep-felt attitude of obedience to Yahweh based upon awe and gratitude, and a manifold system of laws derived from social processes acting upon those feelings of awe and gratitude. The personal experience and religion of the early Yahwists naturally led many persons to respond gladly to the will of Yahweh as they understood it. When that will was recounted in the laws of the Torah as ethical commands from a god known only in tradition as almighty and compassionate, obedience could be interpreted or experienced as oppression under the law. The essential distinction between personal imperative and institutional ethic, then, is one of motivation and interpretation.

Even for those who were socialized into Hebrew religion but had codifying experiences of Yahweh's presence, Yahweh's will was an imperative toward action, not a legalistic demand to obey. Perhaps this realization explains the apparent and recurrent need for the Hebrew people to establish relational contact with Yahweh experientially in each new generation. The Old Testament account reflects the necessary experiential basis of the covenant relationship as it insists each of the patriarchs had his own hierophany (Gen. 17:1-14 for Abraham, 26:1-5 for Isaac, and 28:10-15 for Jacob). Then came Moses' experience related in Exodus 3 and 4 and the Sinai experience in Exodus 20 and 24. Yet in spite of Moses' formative experience and the codifying experience at Sinai, we read in Joshua 24 of the necessity, centuries later, of encouraging Yahweh's people to reaffirm their covenant with Yahweh. Recognizing the difference between Yahwism as a personal piety and Yahwism as a social institutionalization of laws accounts for the prophets who called the Hebrews back to their covenant relationship and many of the Pharisees who continually preached adherence to the Torah and their interpretation of the Torah. Yet there were prophets, like Micah, who preserved the personal, existential imperative of early Yahwism: "and what does the Lord require of you but to do justice, and to love kindness, and to walk humbly with your God?" (Mic. 6:8).

Only those who felt the love and power of Yahweh would sense the required imperative to love and to be humble in the spirit of Micah's admonition. For those reared in early Yahwism (or in later Jewish faith) devoid of any codifying experience, pious demands such as Micah's would appear as laws to be obeyed, not as impulses toward action.

The Interior Love of Early Christianity

To speak of the early Christian impulse to love requires some linguistic and conceptual backpedaling in time. Contemporary notions of love are hardly monolithic, as they range from the flower children's "natural" love to the persistent and pervasive romantic notions that have lit with moonlight and soft music many Hollywood sets in mid-twentieth-century America. The love spread by those persons whose bodies bore paint and flowers emphasized the return to free and natural emotions. Deep involvement with other persons based upon unattached self-sharing was a hallmark of this natural love. It called for freedom in dress (nudity was preferred), in sexual relationships (no selfish claims to one person, as the marriage contract implies), and in emotions (say what you think—do not hide natural emotions behind social politeness). The basic attempt of this love was to live as naturally as possible— that is:

> We want tremendous freedom; we want to be so free that we could just flap our arms and fly through the air. . . . We want to be understood—fully comprehended by others, and to comprehend them fully and not only people but also the rest of creation. We want to be free to be fully open and honest about everything with everyone. We want to be completely free of guilt and shame so that we could even be naked in the presence of others and find it natural. . . . We also long to have children and bring them up in an environment where they will be loved and cared for by all.[21]

In a quite different vein, romantic love, as exemplified in American-made movies of the 1950s and in perennial romanticists of the same culture, is a caricature of social ideals regarding love. Characterized by infatuation (e.g., "I could have danced all night"), romantic love is found in some stereotypes of actors and actresses who epitomize American cultural values. For example, the movie wife of the 1950s was often a dependent, middle-class scatter-brain whose basic claim to importance was her lovability and capacity to bear children (though such an event always occurred behind closed doors). On the other hand,

the male leads were virile men with double-standards—
strong and faithful husbands, except when they cheated a
bit on bowling nights! Even the tragedies were beautiful
in pictures where romantic love endured divorce, wars,
and death itself. While the flower children's love chooses
natural prototypes to emulate, romantic love chooses
social stereotypes.

The above summary of two conflicting notions of love is
not intended to repudiate whatever worth lies in these
two different conceptualizations. Rather, the intention is
to point to the wide semantic range attributed to the word
"love" in American culture. As I try to unfold the force of
the Christian imperative to love, it is important to
recognize the quite different context and range of that
conception in first-century Palestine. Living in a Hellenized part of the world, Palestine's people were exposed
to at least three Greek words that were used to convey the
different experiences the English language packs into the
one word "love." *Eros* indicated what we know as carnal
love; *philos* signified the deep relationship of "brothers";
and *agape* generally connoted affection and concern in
any human relationship. *Philos* and *agape* are the Greek
words used by the Christian scriptures with respect to
Jesus' message, and they gain their specific semantic
value in the interpretation of Jesus as divine love
incarnate (e.g., John 3:16-21 and I John 4:7-10). It is this
interpretation of love—as divine love that gives of itself in
concern for others—that constitutes the early Christian
existential imperative. Therefore, what is difficult to erase
from any early Christian notion of love is the attachment
of sacred (as opposed to natural or social) implications to
its meaning. What the early Christians claim is that they
experienced God's love in their experience of the man
Jesus. Consequently, any command to love is placed in the
context of *responding* to the experience of being loved

first by the Sacred, God. For example, the small epistle of I John states as apodictic:

> Beloved, let us love one another; for love is of God, and he who loves is born of God and knows God. He who does not love does not know God; for God is love. In this the love of God was made manifest among us, that God sent his only Son into the world, so that we might live through him. In this is love, not that we loved God but that he loved us and sent his Son to be the expiation for our sins. (I John 4:7-10)

Another confessional description of Jesus that reveals the impact he had on his early disciples is captured in the book of Acts 10:38, which says, "God anointed Jesus of Nazareth with the Holy Spirit and with power; . . . he went about doing good and healing all that were oppressed by the devil, for God was with him." Jesus was characterized as a good shepherd, kind master, righteous teacher, Son of God, Son of man, and other such affectionate and respectful epithets. It seems that the early Christians felt that Jesus not only taught love as a great commandment, but that he *was* loving.

Still, Jesus did preach as the central ethical command a love of God and of other persons. Matthew captures Jesus' core teaching in the context of a question raised by a young Jew:

> And one of them, a lawyer, asked him a question, to test him. "Teacher, which is the great commandment in the law?" And he said to him, "You shall love the Lord your God with all your heart, and with all your soul, and with all your mind. This is the great and first commandment. And a second is like it, You shall love your neighbor as yourself. On these two commandments depend all the law and the prophets." (Matt. 22:35-40)

This teaching of Jesus was new not in its formulation, but in its application. Jesus was a Jew, and very little of what he said or encouraged had not already been expressed or enjoined in the Hebrew scriptures.[22]

What made Jesus' treatment of old ideas new and different for his disciples was their experience of Jesus' personal application of the love he taught. The result was the rise of love as a responsive impulse in the disciples and followers (e.g., I John 4:7-12). Before love was reduced to an ethical demand, it was encouraged as an intention or motivation that could direct all behavior. In the well-known Sermon on the Mount, Jesus says,

> You have heard that it was said to the men of old, "You shall not kill; and whoever kills shall be liable to judgment." But I say to you that every one who is angry with his brother shall be liable to judgment. (Matt. 5:21-22a)

As the "but I say to you" section of Matthew unfolds, it becomes clear that his disciples understand Jesus' main concern to be to evoke a loving response from the total person (i.e., to alter intentions as well as behavior). Therefore, a key to understanding the early Christian notion of love is to recognize it as an all-pervasive attitude or disposition applied consistently, not a rule of conduct applied only to friends. The most straightforward presentation of this radical interpretation of love is the claim that enemies as well as friends should be loved:

> You have heard that it was said, "You shall love your neighbor and hate your enemy." But I say to you, Love your enemies and pray for those who persecute you, so that you may be sons of your Father who is in heaven; ... For if you love those who love you, what reward have you? Do not even the tax collectors do the same? ... You, therefore, must be perfect, as your heavenly Father is perfect. (Matt. 5:43-48)

Jesus' extreme interpretation of the parameters of love forms the basis for the parable of the good Samaritan, which is told in the context of the two great commandments in the Gospel of Luke (10:25-37). Such a love is certainly not a "natural" love that encourages loving when one feels like it and hating when one feels like it. To some extent, Jesus' love was understood to be a love that transcended worldly or natural impulses—namely, it is like God's love. Furthermore, this "unnatural" love is not a romantic stereotype, but rather follows the divine model of the god-man Jesus. Simply put, "Jesus taught a single basic attitude. . . . Christian love means to do good as Jesus did." [23]

In describing the early Christian community as reported in the book of Acts, Millar Burrows concludes:

> While the word "love" does not occur in Acts, the whole atmosphere of the life of the early church is one of radiant joy and fellowship. . . . In general the attitude toward God commended by the New Testament may be characterized as reverent love. [24]

Love, for Jesus, required a transformation of intention. Therefore, the two commandments of love are sufficient for any particular human situation. Burrows summarizes this conclusion:

> Jesus, agreeing with some of the leading rabbis, puts these two commandments above all the written and oral law. He differs from Deuteronomy and all the rabbis, however, in regarding these two basic commandments as making unnecessary any detailed, specific prescriptions. For him the inner disposition takes precedence over the specific act, though to be sure the right disposition also produces right acts and is judged accordingly. [25]

The apostle Paul asserts, in a similar way, the primary import of love being a product of the "new life" of faith that can result in freedom from the law. He says in Rom. 13:10, "Love does no wrong to a neighbor; therefore love is the fulfilling of the law." Or again, in Gal. 5:14, "For the

141

whole law is fulfilled in one word, 'You shall love your neighbor as yourself.'" Yet in spite of Paul's insistence on the all-sufficient nature of love, he engages in the social process of applying the love-command to specific problems and issues and thereby creates for the institution specific ethical directives. Consider Paul's enumeration of the fruits of the spirit in Gal. 5:22-24. What precedes that list is a series of "ought nots" called "works of the flesh," which carry the force of negative ethical commands (Gal. 5:19-21). Even further evidence of the social application of the love imperative or impulse is Paul's very specific accounting of loving and nonloving behavior in his long love passage in I Corinthians 13. In such love passages, the love impulse is spelled out as an objectified and prescribed ethic. As Paul continues to discuss the "aims of love" in the following chapter (I Corinthians 14), he tackles the apparently widespread practice of speaking in tongues. In that context, he urges limited use of that fruit of the spirit while forbidding any woman to speak at all in the churches. Surely the Puritan practice of segregation of the sexes and the need of women to wear a head covering in the church can be said to follow the Christian ethics prescribed by Paul. However, it is just as clear that such institutional demands are of a different realm and authority than the imperative to love, from which they circuitously descend.

It is necessary, therefore, to make a distinction between personal impulse and piety on the one hand and institutional righteousness on the other. Paul's commands regarding marriage (I Corinthians 7) must be seen to be at least as much a product of his eschatological hope and conviction (i.e., a belief popular in his culture and in his day—cf. I Corinthians 15) as a proclamation arising from the Christian impulse to love. The ethics of the early Christian church were not free from cultural or social influences. However, the basic impulse to love as God loves was not simply a product of mother Judaism. We can explain the Christian love *ethic* to a great extent by the notion of the social construction of realities, but the essential character of the love *imperative* would be missed without a recognition of the early community's experience of being loved by the Sacred through a man named Jesus. In the latter instance, the imperative may be viewed as a function of the experience of being loved. Richard Hiers recognizes this difference between inwardness of disposition and the outwardness of behavior in his delineation of love as "radical obedience" and as command:

> The relevance of Jesus and his ethics is not confined, then, to the "commandment" or "principle" of love. . . . Love involves the subject or self. . . . Love is not simply obedience to requirement: in love as *radical* obedience, one *desires* the well-being of the other person.[26]

Buddha's Detached Compassion

Two seemingly contradictory impulses emerge in early monastic Buddhism as directives to proper behavior. On the one hand, the Buddha's assessment and experience of the world impelled him to renounce the world. This led the Buddha to teach cessation of desire (*nirodha*) as the pivotal imperative leading to nonattachment to the world and its enticements. On the other hand, Buddha's compassion toward all persons was evidenced by his efforts to teach his path to others, regardless of their social position or economic status. Consequently, compassion (Pāli: *mettā* and *karuṇā*) toward others was encouraged by the Buddha as the axial mental disposition to further advancement along the path to perfection. Stories contained in the Pāli Canon represent examples of both imperatives. Let us begin with the tale alluded to earlier of an extremely detached monk:

> A beautiful, young woman married a man of high status and wealth. One morning after a quarrel with her husband, the young wife dressed herself in her finest clothes, added make-up and perfume until she was irresistible, and, then, set out for her family's home.
>
> While on her way, the runaway wife met a Buddhist monk before whom she flaunted her beauty. The monk looked up at her and then continued on his way.
>
> Shortly thereafter, the young girl's husband met the monk and asked if he had seen a pretty young woman on the road. The *bhiksu* replied: "Was it a woman, or a man that passed this way? I cannot tell. But this I know, a set of bones is traveling upon this road."[27]

Such stories as this are told to aspirants on the Buddha's path as they are encouraged to see in the living bodies that walk upon the earth the same impermanence so obvious in rotting, dead bodies.[28]

A detached perception of other persons seems to imply clearly a noninvolvement with people and a removal of oneself from concern for other persons' plights. Yet the stories about the Buddha himself indicate his deep concern and compassion for persons with very worldly needs:

> One account tells how the Buddha once found a monk suffering from dysentery who lay in his own filth. With the aid of Ananda he washed him with his own hands and laid him on a couch. On this occasion he gave the teachings, "Monks, you have not a mother, you have not a father who might tend you. . . . Whoever, monks, would tend me, he should tend the sick."[29]

The Buddha demonstrated his compassion not only for his mendicant brothers; in the famous *jataka*, or "birth tales," a recurring theme is the Buddha's compassionate nature in birth after birth for the benefit of all types and classes of people.[30] How can we understand the relationship between the two seemingly irreconcilable attitudes of detachment and compassion?

To fathom the imperative of nonattachment, the experiences of Gautama are instructive. The life of Gautama took a dramatic turn with his renunciation; and the story of the four visions, to be explored in the next chapter, is a later mythic rationalization of that event. Gautama renounced the pleasures of the *saṃsāra* world prior to his enlightenment. Yet, in the context of his ecstatic illumination, the newborn Buddha is said to have experienced the very flux or impermanence *(anitya)* of corporal existence, from which he concluded that any attachment to this world is an occasion of suffering *(duḥkha)*. Even the notion of self was abandoned *(anātman)* as a transitory perception.

It appears that the immediate experience of the Buddha provided the impelling force and intuitive verification for his attitude of nonattachment to the world that his renunciation had signaled. To assume that such an experience would naturally lead to complete withdrawal from the world and its people, however, is to misunderstand the Buddha's logic with regard to living in the world. As Drummond says,

The Buddha's was the middle way. He taught a radical rejection of phenomenal existence not for the purpose of abandoning it, for even the life of a monk is but another, although presumably better, more efficient mode of living in relation to phenomenal existence. The crux of the matter is the kind of relationship.[31]

For the Buddha, detachment was primarily a mental disposition, not a physical event. Consequently, nonattachment was perceived to be a condition of the mind characterized by selflessness and an absence of desire for worldly objects and enjoyments. Such a cessation of craving was thought to end the suffering connected with saṃsāric existence.[32] The life of attachment (i.e., grasping) to be overcome is described graphically by the Pāli texts:

> Birth is painful, old age is painful, death is painful, grief, lamentation, suffering, misery and despair are painful, painful is it not to get what is wished for, in a word, the Five Groups [mental and physical components of a person] that arise from Grasping are connected with pain.[33]

The notion of nonattachment to the world of suffering, however, does not preclude a positive and controlled system of behavior by which one can achieve that detachment. In fact, the Buddha argues, it is upon the basis of friendly kindness (mettā) that the way to nonattachment is founded.

The discipline that leads to the cessation of desire is called the noble eightfold path and comprises the fourth noble truth. Right view, right intention, right speech, right action, right livelihood, right effort, right mindfulness, and right concentration are the eight spokes to this wheel of dhamma, or duty.[34]

Early commentators grouped the eight stages into three categories of discipline, which constitute an ascending order of perfection: śīla, or moral conduct, includes right speech, action, and livelihood; samādhi, or concentration, embraces right mindfulness, effort, and concentration; and prajñā, or intuitive insight, contains right view and intention.[35] The ordering in the Pāli text is more instructive, however. The first two concepts, right view and right intention, serve as the conceptual basis for the remaining six. Right view, according to the text, is knowledge and acceptance of the four noble truths. The text describes right view this way: "Knowledge, bhik-khus, about Ill [dukkha], knowledge about the coming to be of Ill, knowledge about the cessation of Ill, knowledge about the Way that leads to the cessation of Ill. This is what is called right view." [36] What the first spoke of the wheel of dhamma expresses, therefore, is the imperative to renounce the world of duḥkha through the direction of the eightfold path. The second spoke, right intention, is a statement of the mental disposition that produces correct knowledge. The text explicitly indicates that the proper disposition is a twofold one of renunciation and kindly concern: "And what is right aspiration [intention]? The aspiration towards renunciation, the aspiration toward benevolence, the aspiration towards kindness. This is what is called right aspiration." [37] Therefore, cessation of the craving that leads to attachment and a benevolent or kindly attitude toward others are the two sides of the coin of proper relationships in the world. While the *negative* imperative leads to detachment from the ephemeral nature of humankind, the *positive* thrust encourages active pursuit of relationships in the world with kindness (mettā) and compassion (karuṇā). As Drummond points out,

> proper thought meant the consistent practice of benevolence [mettā] toward all beings, active concern for their welfare, and a tranquility of mind . . . characterized by alertness and energy of mind. . . . Such thought is also characterized by friendship with [or aspiration for] that which is lovely, which in one passage is equated with the whole of the Noble Eightfold Path.[38]

The experiential source of the Buddhist emphasis on compassion or friendly concern for others seems to have been twofold. First of all, the Buddha appears to have taught this quality as a truth given in his Nirvāṇic experience. In the second place, his early disciples say they experienced the Buddha's very willingness to teach his path as an act of compassion. G. C. Pande notes, "Out of compassion . . . Buddha agreed to preach his gospel. He is called 'compassionate towards all beings' and with the lapse of centuries his followers emphasized this aspect of this teaching more and more."[39]

Buddha's formulation of the compassion ethic was possibly informed by the ubiquitous teaching of his day called the Brahma-viharas ("divine states" of mind), which listed as the four exalted virtues: lovingkindness, compassion, sympathetic joy, and equanimity.[40] Yet, whatever the social influences, it appears to have been his illuminating experience of Nirvāṇa that led the Buddha to stress concerned kindness toward others. Even more, it is clear that the disciples' experience of the Buddha as a compassionate person in their midst could have led to the centrality of that imperative. In summarizing the twofold impulses of early Buddhism, Rahula says,

> According to Buddhism for a man to be perfect there are two qualities that he should develop equally: compassion (karuṇā) on one side, and wisdom (pannā) on the other. Here compassion represents love, charity, kindness, tolerance and such noble qualities on the one side, or qualities of the heart while wisdom would stand for the intellectual side or qualities of the mind.[41]

What was the key to the paradoxical impulses (nonattachment and compassion) of early Buddhism? It was the realization by the Buddha that it is not only right actions that make a person righteous, but also right intentions. Furthermore, only when the mind is kindly directed can attachments stemming from self-centered desire be overcome. This leads the Buddha to encourage persons to have a kindly attitude toward others as a corrective to passionate or angry attachments to those same persons. A later canonical text called the Dhammapada summarizes many of the ethical teachings of the early Buddhist community. This text explains the need and result of kindly concern (mettā) in its opening lines:

> All that we are is the result of what we have thought: it is founded on our thoughts, it is made up of our thought. If a man speaks or acts with an evil thought, pain follows him, as the wheel follows the foot of the ox that draws the wagon.
>
> If a man speaks or acts with a pure thought, happiness follows him, like a shadow that never leaves him.
>
> For never does hatred cease by hatred here below: hatred ceases by love; this is an eternal law.[42]

The goal of the eightfold path, therefore, is to overcome particular kinds of attachments—namely those which arise from self-centered desiring or craving. To reach this goal, the aspirant must focus his or her attention on kindly disposed actions that root out any negative attitudes and thoughts that are at the base of attached actions and overcome the dominant interest in oneself. Consequently, kindly concern or compassion is encouraged as a positive intention of the mind, not as a passionate attachment to other persons. The one who is wise should see a bag of bones in the beauty of the flesh, and the one who has right intentions should respond with equanimity to the needs of others. In other words, the one who would follow the Buddha must have detached compassion as the impulse for all his or her actions.

The ethics of Theravada Buddhism are but an application of the twofold impulse of detached compassion to worldly events, persons, and situations. The fivefold set of Buddhist precepts represents one such application of detached compassion. These ethical commands share the general thrust of the non-Buddhist ethical systems of the same period in India, as they include: (1) non-injury (ahiṃsā) to any creature; (2) non-stealing; (3) abstinence from sexual contact; (4) refraining from false speech; and

(5) abstinence from use of intoxicating beverages. The Buddhist *saṅgha* appended five additional precepts, which prohibited: (1) eating at forbidden times; (2) dancing, singing, etc.; (3) adornment of the body with perfumes, garlands, etc.; (4) using a chair or seat; and (5) receiving or using gold and silver.[43] In all ten precepts, the desire to overcome attachment to the world (perfumes, gold, etc.) is balanced by the intent to treat with kindly concern other persons (non-injury, non-stealing, etc.). The ten commands objectify the two-sided impulse of detached compassion.

In Buddha's day there were other mendicant groups that stressed nonattachment to the world as the primal religious drive (*e.g.,* the Jains). However, no other group contemporary with the Buddha's seems to have balanced the world-negating impulse of detachment with the positive desire for compassionate concern that made the Buddha's path truly a Middle Way. Detached compassion serves as the proper mental and emotional foundation for the moral actions (right speech, action, and livelihood) and mental disciplines (right effort, mindfulness, and concentration) of the eightfold path of the Buddha.

Summary Comments

Behavior can reveal the attitudes and intentions of a person in a way that words do not. Consequently, conduct frequently becomes the yardstick against which a person's stated convictions are judged. As the result of a personal religious experience, a person is more apt to act in accord with what he or she claims to believe, because such experiences have the power to alter intentions as well as convictions. In the realm of personal religion, therefore, proper behavior may consistently result from impulses originating in experiences of Sacred Power. For example, the decision to keep Yahweh's covenant was, for some

Hebrews, a matter of enacting in behavior feelings of gratitude and awe arising from the Exodus experience. In another context, the behavior of many early Christians seems to have been guided by an experience of being loved that led to an inner disposition to love. In still another environment, selfless concern for others marked by emotional detachment was a motivating force for those who encountered Nirvāṇic calm. Religious imperatives, therefore, may differ in content, but do operate to inform the intentions as well as the conceptions of a religious experiencer.

In the realm of social religiosity, a person is usually taught what constitutes ethical or proper behavior. In this context, ethics are learned conceptions born of the social process and its experiences. Consequently, the learned ethic may be perceived as an imposed demand. Yet even when voluntarily accepted, ethics represent acquired norms of behavior often without any personal desire to actualize them. For example, the laws of Yahweh's covenant became for many Hebrews legalistic impositions. Likewise, the Christian commandment to love one's enemies could be rejected more easily in the face of persecution by a hated Roman army. Finally, the disputes on dietary and comfort rules of the sangha by the Mahāsaṅghikas indicate that some early Buddhist monks felt the requirements associated with the life of the monk's assembly were too constricting. In short, ethical requirements associated with social forms of religiosity often represented objects of controversy instead of emulation. Consequently, what for one person may be an imperative born of experience becomes for another a legalistic shackle.

Chapter 5
Religious Reflection and World Construction

Thesis

Just as physical behavior may be viewed from the different vantage points of personal and social religion, so too may mental behavior—namely, reflection. As we saw earlier, when an ecstatic religious experience occurs, mythic attempts to express and ritual efforts to re-create emerge. Furthermore, the "sacralized" person usually feels impelled to act in accord with the received illumination or insight. It is not long, however, until the "reborn" person begins to reflect on the broader significance of his or her experience. Sometimes this reflection occurs immediately upon receiving a dramatic experience, while at other times a span of time separates the initial experience from full questioning and reflection. I have called the narratives that express or relate the sacred encounter *expressive* myths. I will call those sacred narratives whose function is explanation and speculation *reflective* myths. With reflective myths, non-narrative ruminations on the Sacred and didactic formulas develop to form a young tradition's germinal theology. The so-called beliefs of a tradition are thereby extended.

Reflective myths arise as an activity homologous to the

development of imperatives and ethics. Therefore, reflective stories and formulations do not long remain the private property of their originators but soon become incorporated into social religion as legitimations of the social religious world view. Consequently, what initially represents a personal attempt to explain or to understand an experience more fully, becomes an institution's creedal statement of the way things really are. One aspect of this process of reflection and legitimizing will now be discussed.

From Reflection to Facticity

Michael Novak states well the nature of sacred scriptures:

> The experience of the sacred is so important to humans that when it occurs they ordinarily wish to preserve it and to repeat it. . . . Liturgical acts re-present the original experience in order to stoke the fires of memory [or create in experience the subject of memory, I would add]. . . . The wisdom pointed to by these basic themes [preserved in memory] is often set forth in writing, in stark simplicity or in intricate commentary. "Sacred texts" arise. . . . Nearly every major world religion is organized, in one way or another, around a set of sacred texts. Original experiences of the sacred lie behind the black print.[1]

Sacred texts usually contain as their essential core: (1) expressive myths that relate in narrative form the founder's contact with the Sacred; (2) core ritual(s) in outline or in full; (3) ethical injunctions and prescriptive behavior; and (4) reflective myths, which attempt to explain (e.g., the origin of the world) and to integrate (e.g., in ethical injunctions or application of ethics) the core religious experience in socially understood concepts.[2]

Reflective myths are essentially second-level or posterior reflection. Such myths are not the immediate expression of a religious experience, but the products of later reflection, which occurs when application of the core experience is attempted. Such applications relate the Sacred to the everyday world, its realities, its problems. In short, reflective myths are a narrative form of theologizing. (In this sense theology is regarded as sustained reflection upon everyday concerns and events in light of a sense of the Sacred). Reflective myths evidence at least three distinct but interrelated purposes and functions: (1) explanation of origins, (2) rationalization, and (3) apology. First of all, reflective myths may explain, and thereby integrate, the beginning of the Sacred's relationship to and involvement in the everyday world. Such myths are often etiological in that they explain the origin of natural or social phenomena. For example, the Hebrew creation myth we shall examine represents the etiological type of reflective myth because it attempts to account for Yahweh's involvement in the genesis of the empirical world. The story of the tower of Babel is also an etiological or explanatory myth that accounts for the social phenomenon of diverse languages.

The second function of reflective myth is to rationalize or explain human problems and concerns in light of the Sacred.[3] These myths attempt to explain not simply the origin of, but also the ongoing involvement of, a Sacred Power in the lives of its people. For example, the persistence of suffering may be explained in the Hebrew context by the story of Adam and Eve as a natural condition of human beings caused by their fall from perfection. The problem of suffering in the classical Indian context is related to the concepts of karma (action) and dharma (duty and cosmic law), which place the Sacred entirely beyond the realm of suffering and make each person responsible for his or her own worldly plight. Though the answers are different, the same problem requires a religious explanation. Another perennial human problem, the threat of death, is rationalized in most religious traditions in light of possible sacred answers. For example, myths describing blissful paradises (Indian or Christian) are one way that religious traditions blunt fears of death, by suggesting human beings are immortal.[4] I shall use the story of Buddha's four visions, or sights, which led to his renunciation of the world, as an example of one answer given to the nature and solution of human finiteness.

The third purpose and function of reflective myths is to explain and defend the personal (and later, institutional) religion before its cultural antagonists. I will use the term "apologetic" (in its Greek sense of "fit for defense") for this function of reflective myth. When confronted with challenges from other social realities—including the everyday reality—religious traditions provide in their apologetic myths a defense of their sacred reality. For example, the story of Elijah's victory over and destruction of four hundred fifty Baal priests through the power of Yahweh is one apologetic response to a Canaanite cult that enjoyed the devotion of many Hebrews in the early days of settlement in Palestine (I Kings 18:17-40). In a different way the writer of the Gospel of John modifies Greek and Hebrew categories into Christian ones as he presents and defends Christianity in a Hellenized land where Greek ideas held sway. A hymnic example from John will be used as an example of apologetic reflection.

In all its functions, reflective myth hearkens back to personal experience as the impetus for and judge of its proclamation. William James describes the psychological process involved:

Articulate reasons are cogent for us only when our inarticulate feelings of reality have already been impressed in favor of the same conclusion. . . . Our impulsive belief is here always what sets up the original body of truth, and our articulately verbalized philosophy is but its showy translation into formulas.[5]

Speaking of the contemporary religious situation, R. D. Laing comments, "We do not need theories so much as the source of the theory. We are not satisfied with faith, in the sense of an implausible hypothesis irrationally held: we demand to experience the 'evidence'."[6] Reflective myths, then, are not implausible hypotheses, but reconsiderations of the core experience in light of external, or internal, challenges and questions. When religious reflections are fashioned by those within the sphere of social religion as its legitimating data, those statements more closely approximate hypotheses that attempt to create social plausibility. This later, socializing activity moves beyond the creation of reflective myths and statements to the formulation of creeds and dogmas codified by institutional, not experiential, sanctions. Unless the theologian writes from a core or a codifying experience, his theology will represent, essentially, reflection upon sacred tradition, not experience. Therefore, theology may represent reflection upon the personal experiences and conclusions of others in order to defend the claims of the socially defined religious reality. Consequently, a second angle from which to view the reasoning process of social religion (i.e., theology) is from the context of plausibility structures and social legitimations.

Viewed sociologically, theology is a secondary socialization process that attempts to maintain the plausibility of a religious reality. If we understand social religion to be just one reality that must compete with other realities for acceptance, we recognize the crucial role theology has for religious institutions. As one of the multiple realities confronting a person, the social form of a religious tradition is conveyed from generation to generation through a mixture of various socialization processes. When a society or culture embraces a particular religious tradition, the transmission of cultural or social values and customs through public media (educational instruction, newspapers, etc.) may also include aspects—however distorted—of social religion. Furthermore, religious instruction is simply one segment of parents' larger task of socializing their children into acceptable mental *and* physical behavior. Still, the most obvious and direct religious socialization process takes place under the auspices of religious institutions (church or school, temple or ashram). We saw earlier that two of the basic functions of religious institutions are the social control of thought and action, and the preservation, in tradition, of the accumulated wisdom of many generations. In order to retain the allegiance of the members of a religious institution and to appeal to potential initiates, the beliefs, norms, and traditions of any religion must seek social plausibility. The process of legitimation, therefore, represents a tertiary process that commonly utilizes more abstract conceptualizations than initial or secondary socialization formulas to convince the skeptical.[7]

If social religion can, to a major extent, be viewed as a socially constructed reality, then the social processes that form, transmit, and preserve that symbolic universe follow a pattern not unlike that of other social universes (e.g., a science or a particular philosophy). Each of these realities arises out of the dialectic between human experience, physical environment, and the social context—that is, out of personal experience *and* social objectification. While primary and secondary socialization processes introduce new members into these social universes, plausibility in them is maintained by the use of legitimations that explain and defend the established reality. Therefore, each social world has its own plausibility structure—namely, a "social base for the suspension of doubt without which the definition of reality in question cannot be maintained in consciousness."[8]

Objectified "knowledge" of any social reality may be transmitted through socialization or learning processes. Subjective acceptance of any reality, however, depends in part upon personal contact with other "believers." In other words, full acquaintance with the factual content of a religious tradition is only a first step. To accept the socially shared religion as "my religion" or "my faith"— that is, as a world important "to me"—is to claim that social universe as a subjective reality. It is the basic task of plausibility structures to provide that subjective, "for me," experience; and it is the religious community that shares that reality which is the social base.[9] The Cuna rite of *Muu Igala* could not function in times of stress if the whole community (mid-wife, singers, shaman, etc.) did not act as a social base of support for the symbolic universe that the pregnant woman uses in her childbirth odyssey. Plausibility structures provide for the initiate an internalization of a symbolic universe, which for outsiders is simply an objective, and often untrue, world of ideas.

Berger and Luckmann call the acceptance of a new symbolic universe "re-socialization" or "transformation."[10] Therefore, religious conversion is, on one level, an occasion of social transformation. The plausibility structure of a religious reality is crucially important because it "must become the individual's world, displacing all other worlds, especially the world the individual 'inhabited' before his alternation."[11] In this process of transformation for a new "convert," the conflict between the adopted religious reality and the everyday reality occurs. Since all religious worlds claim a Sacred reality that is ultimately the most meaningful and eternally real, the social and natural world of everyday perception is, by definition, devalued.[12] When this conflict occurs, challenges are brought to the seemingly exaggerated claims of religion.

The need for legitimating formulas continues even beyond the initial conversion of members in order to meet these challenges. Theological myths and statements, therefore, may be viewed as the legitimating formulas of social religion.[13] Such legitimations are the "socially objectivated 'knowledge' that serves to explain and justify the social order."[14] Because all socially constructed, as well as personally impelled, social realities are competing for recognition with other universes of knowledge, legitimations are necessary on every level of the socialization process. On one level, there is the "self-legitimating facticity" of the elements of knowledge passed on in primary socialization. On another level of conceptual abstraction, the full-blown concepts and creeds of religion attempt to persuade the convert by theoretical construction and integration.[15] These latter are the secondary legitimations that in social religion are called theology. Consequently, as "'second-order' objectification of meaning," theological formulations attempt to maintain the plausibility of the social religious reality.

Berger and Luckmann call legitimations the "conceptual machinery" of universe maintenance.[16] In noting a progression of more and more sophisticated symbolic universes, they place mythology as the most naïve and least theoretical. In their scheme, theology is paradigmatic for later philosophical and scientific conceptualizations of the cosmos as it tries to account for the whole cosmos in its symbolic universe. Therefore, theological thinking serves to mediate between everyday reality and the Sacred reality expressed in myth. Because theology is intended essentially to explain and to defend a religious reality to skeptics and apostates, it utilizes in its rebuttal the symbols, conceptions, and language of its detractors. Therefore, while theology is "closer to mythology in the religious contents of its definitions of reality, it is closer to the later secularized conceptions [i.e., philosophy and science] in its social location." [17]

On an empirical level, the very existence of alternative realities demonstrates that a religiously conceived universe is less than inevitable. [18] Furthermore, nonreligious symbolic universes attempt to account for the same phenomena in their secularized and systematic "knowledge" that personal and social religion sacralize in their formulations. Any attempts to label as true or false the conflicting claims to knowledge have as much to do with one's culture, subculture, personal experiences, and taste as they do with objective or subjective reasoning or logic. Berger and Luckmann put it this way:

> What remains sociologically essential is the recognition that all symbolic universes and all legitimations are human products; their existence has its base in the lives of concrete individuals, and has no empirical status apart from these lives. [19]

Just as reflective myths explain, rationalize, and defend, so too later theology takes up these tasks for generations not a part of the germinal community. If reflective myths may be described as sustained reflection on religious experience, we should be aware that the impetus for such cogitation arises from everyday human experience. Theology may arise from the need to explain codifying religious experiences within social religious tradition, or from everyday human questions and concerns.[20] Consequently, reflective myths and theology may represent extended explications of religious experience(s) or deliberations upon human problems in need of religious answers. The further removed from immediate experience(s) reflections arise, the more they engage themselves in the issues and conceptual battles of other social realities (e.g., the battle between evolutionists and biblical literalists). Consequently, chronological *and experiential* distance often separates a theologian from the founding experience. Theology composed from such a distance can be expected to evidence contemporary social concerns, if not attitudes.

In summary, the religious realm of personal experience and that of social process intermingle again, on the level of religious constructs or legitimations. The weight of influence here, however, is not equal, since reflective myths and theology are far more the product of the mind than of the emotions. Likewise, such myths are more the product of social systems (especially language) than of personal experience. *It is in the beliefs, creeds, and reflective thinking of social religion that personal religion may become smothered in the verbiage created by the mind. Yet it is also in the reflective formulations that emotional excesses can be checked.* While theologizing may be a secondary reflective process, it is crucial to the plausibility structure of social religion. Furthermore, reflective myths and formulations are important to personal religion in their integrative and explanatory roles of presenting experience in an intelligible way. Such formulations give structure and form to feelings and impressions. Whether initial reflection or apologetic conceptualization, reflective myths and statements are essential ingredients of both personal and social religion.

Hebrew Creation

Two major creation motifs already present in the Eastern Mediterranean cultures prior to the arrival of the Moses tribes focused, on the one hand, on the natural, vegetation (seasonal) cycle of birth, death, and rebirth and, on the other hand, on the cosmic struggle between forces of watery chaos and creative order.[21] The dying/rising god theme occurred in several cultures of the ancient Near East, including the previous Egyptian homeland of the Moses tribes. Still, that dying/rising motif seems not to have influenced those Hebrews responsible for the maintenance and development of Hebrew oral or written traditions (even though some laymen seem to have been attracted to the Baal cult, as indicated by the story of Elijah and Baal priests). Rather, the symbols connected with creation from a watery chaos informed the official Hebrew speculation about the origin of the world.

A general assumption shared by most Near Easterners from 3000 B.C. to Moses' day was that the universe consisted of three distinct regions or spheres.[22] The upper realm consisted of the heavens of the gods; a flat disc composed of dirt and rock and supported by pillars or mountains comprised the human abode; while the underworlds encompassed both chaotic waters and dry, barren realms for the dead. A firmament, or sky-dome, separated the heavenly waters from the earth disc, which was in constant danger of being deluged by waters from above or below. It is the creation of such a universe that both the Akkadian and Gen. 1:1–2:4a creation stories tell.

The Akkadian myth is commonly called the *Enūma elish* ("When on high," the opening words of the story). It tells first of the creation of the gods by the primordial pair, Tiamat ("salty water") and Apsu ("sweet water"). In a family quarrel, the younger gods kill their father before he can destroy them. Their mother, Tiamat, vows revenge on her children, and the great struggle between the primordial, destructive power of the salt waters and the controlling power of the ruling gods is initiated. Marduk, the youngest of the divine children, is chosen to represent all the gods as their lord after he demonstrates his creative might by causing a piece of cloth to vanish and to reappear by verbal command. Armed with various weapons given him by his godly benefactors, Marduk defeats Tiamat and kills her. Splitting Tiamat in half, Marduk constructs the heavenly vault from one half of Tiamat and places in the firmament constellations of stars, which form the heavenly calendar. From the second half of Tiamat, the earth and its foundations are formed. The only task remaining is to mass together blood and bones to form the first humans. Therefore, it is from the blood of one of Tiamat's warriors, Kingu, that the first human beings are made.[23]

It is not difficult to see similarities between the Akkadian myth of Tiamat and the Priestly tradition's story, contained in Gen. 1:1–2:4a. In the Priestly (P) story, the creation of the heavenly beings is not mentioned; but the first word picture that is painted is of a primordial, desolate sea over which ranges the spirit of God (Gen. 1:2). That the Hebrew image of a primordial sea is not likely an innocent coincidence with the Tiamat image of the Akkadian myth is demonstrated by Ringgren when he explains that the Hebrew word used in Gen. 1:2 for sea is tᵉhom, which is etymologically linked to the Babylonian word tiāmat.[24] Furthermore, as the creation of the world unfolds, the firmament (sky-dome), dry land, and heavenly measurements of time (sun, moon, and stars) closely resemble the world model of the Enūma elish.

Another similarity of the two myths, though not emphasized equally, is the use of creative speech. Yahweh tames the primeval waters and creates the material, animal, and human components of the world by acts of speech alone. Stressing these mighty verbal acts, a later psalmist says, "For he spoke and it came to be; he commanded, and it [the world] stood forth" (Ps. 33:9). The Akkadian parallel occurs when Marduk demonstrates his divine powers by verbally calling into being a piece of cloth (after causing it to disappear). It is the case in the Akkadian myth, however, that Marduk constructed the world out of the primordial waters (Tiamat) he defeated in battle with angry winds and arrows, not with his words. It is Yahweh's complete reliance on his creative word that gives the Genesis 1 account a very different thrust from Marduk's incidental use of divine speech.[25]

A major innovation of the Genesis 1 story is the temporal framework given creation by placing the eight acts of creation in six days. On the seventh day God rested. While many creation myths in the ancient Near East include calendrical time-keeping as a product of creation, the Priestly story in Genesis uses a seven-day time-frame in which the creation process itself occurs. It should not be surprising that scholars have dated this Hebrew story in the seventh or sixth century B.C., when the seven-day (Sabbath) ritual calendar had become commonplace in Hebrew worship.[26] Yet another feature of the Genesis 1 story that sets it off from its contemporary counterparts is the central place given to mankind as the focus of the creation process. Unlike the Akkadian myth, the Priestly story highlights human beings, male and female, as the only products of creation fashioned in the image of God (or the heavenly beings—Gen. 1:27). Furthermore, it is to this exalted, though not divine, mankind that God gave the responsibility of governing all other products of creation, animal and vegetable (Gen. 1:28).[27]

Up to this point I have focused upon the Genesis 1 story as though it were the only creation story found in the Hebrew traditions. Such is not the case. For if one reads further in Genesis, a second story of the creation of mankind unfolds (2:4b ff.). In this second story, usually ascribed to the Yahwist (J) tradition, a desert, not a primeval sea, exists prior to God's creative activity. The first "act" of creation is the appearance of a mist that rises up from the ground, nourishing the desert and making life possible (Gen. 2:5-6).

In a decidedly anthropomorphic vein, the story of Genesis 2 continues with the creation of man (adam in Hebrew) formed from the dust of the earth and enlivened by the breath of God (Gen. 2:7). In reverse fashion to the Priestly story, only after man is formed does God cause trees, rivers, and animals to come forth and join the man in the oasis called Eden. When all other creatures fail to provide companionship for the lonely man, God creates a woman from one of the ribs of the man (Gen. 2:21-23). The Yahwist story begins and ends with the creation of man and woman. The fact that there is no mention of the creation of the heavens and earth has led Gerhard von Rad to say that the Yahwist story is not a creation myth at all.[28] Yet von Rad does acknowledge that the Priestly and Yahwist stories are alike in that they both focus on the creation of mankind (though in their own ways) and "that the rest of the world is ordered round them (male and female) as the chief work of Yahweh in Creation."[29]

It is very likely that the P and J stories did not receive their present form until the sixth or seventh century B.C.[30] Nonetheless, it is not likely that the early Moses tribes could have lived for long near the Canaanite people, with their fertility religion centering around Baal and the high god El, and not have had to deal with the questions of creation and fertility themselves. Ringgren suggests that when the Canaanite high god (and creator god) El was assimilated into Hebrew theology, it is probable that Yahweh too would have been considered a creator god.[31] On the one hand, it would seem that the two creation stories found in Genesis depended heavily upon the prevailing cosmological motifs of the ancient Near East. On the other hand, it is clear that the Hebrews did not simply borrow wholesale the extant creation motifs they used, but rather transformed borrowed mythological conceptions into stories that fit their understanding and experience of Yahweh.

It is not as easy as it first appears to explain *why* the Hebrew creation stories were written. The obvious answer is that they were formulated as theoretical explanations of the origin of the world and mankind. However, while scholars vary widely in their own explanation, many agree in dismissing such a simplistic response. Ringgren says that the primary purpose of the creation narratives is "to illustrate the enduring result of creation . . . (that is) the absolute dependence of all that lives upon Yahweh."[32] Ludwig Kohler agrees that the major reason for the composing of the creation stories in Genesis was not speculation about the birth of the world but an answer to the question, From where does the history of God's people derive its meaning?[33] According to Kohler it is the Yahweh experienced in the Exodus and his power that is being described, not the creation of the world. Fohrer, agreeing that Yahweh's credibility is at stake, feels the impetus for the creation stories was competition from the Canaanite god Baal. He says, "For Palestinian Yahwism the crucial question was to whom the Israelite farmer owed the fertility of his fields: Yahweh or the Canaanite god Baal."[34]

Consistent in all the above interpretations is the insistence that the creation narratives in Genesis are not simply etiological stories that explain the origin of the world. To be sure, they do serve that function. But, more important, the borrowed myths have been transformed consistently to reveal the same god at work in creation who was experienced in the Exodus journey from Egypt. For example, the creation motifs are utilized by the Psalmists and Deutero-Isaiah as signs that Yahweh always has acted on behalf of his people Israel (e.g., Psalms 89 and 104; Isa. 54:5). This leads von Rad to conclude that "presumptuous as it may sound, Creation is a part of the aetiology of Israel."[35] In other words, the creation of the world (as recounted in Genesis) is understood by the Psalmists and Deutero-Isaiah as another example of the saving power of the Yahweh who was experienced in the Exodus and the calling together of the nation Israel.

One way to understand the creation stories of Genesis, then, is to see them as reflections upon questions of origins from the perspective of the Exodus experience and faith. In this instance, the Genesis stories are assumed to represent the transformation of borrowed creation myths into witnesses of Yahweh's might and power.[36] Anderson best summarizes the nature of the transformation that stamps the Hebrew understanding of Yahweh upon mythical ideas current in other forms in the ancient Near East:

> The creation accounts at the beginning of the Bible are written from the standpoint of the meaning disclosed in the Exodus. The history that is now recorded forwards must be read backwards, so to speak, through the faith of the believing community. And the fulcrum of Israel's faith . . . is the event of the Exodus. In a profound sense the Bible does not really begin with Genesis but with Exodus.[37]

We can find in the cultures surrounding ancient Palestine creation motifs and myths similar to those found in Genesis. However, what we also find in Genesis, that is missing in the myths of Baal or Marduk, is the transformation of creation from a cosmic event to a personal event occurring in a people's history. Many scholars deduce from this analysis that such a modification "historicizes" earlier myths. For example, Ringgren states the proposition this way: "Mythological material has been placed in a historical framework. The creation is the beginning of history; the deluge is an event in the history of mankind."[38] Such attempts to claim for the Hebrew creation stories a historical character does point to one "innovation" offered in the Genesis myths: the cyclical time of the dying/rising gods is replaced with a linear history, or time, of Yahweh's people that has a beginning point and an end.[39] Nonetheless, the word "history" must be redefined to include the event of a god, a Sacred, whose mode of action entails historical and natural events.

It is no less problematic, from the secularist's point of view, that the Hebrews claim to have experienced Yahweh in historical events (including the creation) than if they had claimed a cosmic event as Yahweh's creation (like the cosmic battle between Marduk and Tiamat). The hurdle for the person who has adopted a nonreligious stance is the assertion that *it was Yahweh* who accomplished the Exodus and creation (not whether Yahweh's actions took place in history or in a cosmic realm). If a myth is a story of a Sacred's activity, either separate from or in relation to humankind, then historical interaction represents only one kind of Sacred activity.

What the creation stories of the Hebrews afford is a recognition of the basic distinction that should be made between expressive myths and reflective myths. The Exodus event (understood cumulatively) provided experiences that gave birth to personal assurance among members of the Moses tribes that Yahweh was their god.

The story of that encounter with their Sacred, found in the book of Exodus, was an attempt to express and explicate that experience. The stories of creation found in Genesis, on the other hand, are the product of reflection upon the question of origin (and, perhaps, fertility) answered from the perspective of the Exodus experience. It is likely that the Genesis creation stories arose chronologically after the Exodus experience gave rise to devotion to Yahweh, and in response to particular challenges (perhaps from Baal or El) or to recurrent questions about the origin of the world. Nonetheless, these reflective myths are stated with the same positive assurance that the expressive myths are. Hebrew creation myths are, in effect, reflective expressions of the faith derived from the Exodus experiences.

One can explain, from the point of view of socialization processes, the dissemination of creation motifs and stories. However, the process of transformation of "foreign" motifs and stories by the Hebrew people is best understood as a product of reflection upon the personal religious experience of the Exodus. While the Genesis stories are etiological myths that explain creation of the world, they are more forcefully expressions of a personal faith that began with the Exodus. The *central purpose* of the Genesis stories is to explain the origin of the relationship between Yahweh and his people, not to describe how the world came into being. In terms of their function in the reflective lore of their day, the P and J stories are not primarily creation myths at all. They are, instead, etiological myths that trace the origin of Yahweh's relationship to the people Israel back to the creation of the world itself.

The Christian Logos or Word

Using a hymnic passage from the Gospel of John, I intend to explicate one example of apologetic reflection.

The hymnic passage of which I speak is the so-called Prologue of John's Gospel (John 1:1-18). What seems at first to be an enigmatic poem utilizing metaphorical language to the extreme is really a reflective narrative or myth relating the biography of the man-God, Jesus. As Raymond E. Brown says, "The Prologue is a description of the history of salvation in hymnic form."[40] What makes the Prologue an especially fruitful passage is that it is, in effect, an introduction to and summary of the whole message of the Gospel of John.[41]

Two notable features of the Gospel of John are (1) the frequency and use of Hellenistic terms and expressions (*logos* is the most controversial of them), and (2) the anti-Jewish bias of many passages that deal with the established Jewish officials and the synagogue (e.g., 3:10; 5:16; 7:14-24; 9:13-23; 16:1-5). These characteristics of the Gospel have led investigators to conclude that its author lived in an area of great Hellenic influence that had strong Jewish settlements.[42] Ephesus of Asia Minor seems the most likely location for the origin of the composition of John. First of all, the early ecclesiastical traditions (especially Irenaeus') almost all agree on that city, and, in the second place, Ephesus had active synagogues (compare the Revelation of John 2:9 and 3:9) and yet was a thoroughly Hellenistic community. The authorship of the Gospel is not certain, although the most likely author is the disciple John, the son of Zebedee.[43] The compilation of the Gospel of John underwent several stages of development, which culminated in a final redaction near the end of the first century (90–100 A.D.).[44]

For our understanding of the hymnic Prologue, two additional features are important to consider. The first aspect is John's metaphorical use of the term "word" (*logos* in Greek), around which the whole Prologue is built. The second trait is the author's use of the dualistic categories "light" and "darkness." These two features led Bultmann to claim Gnostic origins of John's thought in general, and the Gnostic redeemer myth for the Prologue in particular.[45] In contrast, Brown and others argue that all of John's terms and conceptualizations derive from the Palestinian Judaism (including Old Testament and Apocalyptic traditions) of Jesus' day.[46]

What the analysis below suggests is that John's use of the term *logos* and his expression of the dualism of light and darkness are not synonymous with *any* previously known tradition, Hebrew or Greek. Furthermore, John's message would have been understandable both to the Christian steeped in the Hebrew traditions, and to the Greek convert or antagonist who would have understood John out of a completely different religious and philosophical background.[47] Whatever parallel or comparative use of terms and conceptions, John was written by a contemplative author who created a mythic and hymnic biography of Jesus quite unlike any other.

The Prologue begins by talking about a "Word," also called "The Light," which both resides with God and *is* God (1:1, 2); and it is not until near the end of the hymn that this "Son from the Father" (vs. 14) is identified with Jesus (vs. 17). What we learn, therefore, is that the author of the Prologue is actually summarizing the life of Jesus. Much in the same way that each of the earlier "biographies" (Matthew, Mark, and Luke) begins with an attempt to place Jesus in an accepted Hebrew context (back to King David, to Isaiah's prophecy, or to the first man, Adam, respectively), the Prologue traces the life of Jesus back prior to the creation of the world. The Prologue reports that Jesus, who was the preexistent Son of God, was the power of God (light and life) by which the whole universe was created (vss. 1-3). Yet, even though he created the whole universe, when he entered the human world he was not recognized or welcomed (vss. 10, 11; cf. vss. 4, 5). But some people did recognize and accept him, and those persons became the spiritual children of God (vss. 12, 13; cf. 3:1-21). It is then repeated for emphasis that "the Word became flesh and dwelt among us"—that is, the preexistent Jesus became the earthly Jesus of Nazareth. But, most important, Jesus' life and ministry were marked by "merciful love" (vs. 14).[48] Therefore, Jesus' life and ministry were a fulfillment of the work God began in Moses (vss. 16-17). In the end, what is important about the man Jesus is that he made God known among mankind. In fact, to know the man Jesus was to know the unseen God himself (vs. 18).[49]

The use of the metaphor Word (*logos*) is one example of John's unique way of restating a story that was known in at least three other forms (i.e., the Synoptic Gospels) to the early Christian communities spread throughout Palestine and Asia Minor. *Logos* was the central concept of Stoic philosophy, and it explained the divine or universal principle that was thought to give order to the mundane world. *Logos* was also the name of the salvific person of the Gnostic redeemer myth.[50] But it is also the case, as we observed in the Priestly creation story, that the Hebrew tradition knows of the power of God's word, by which he created the world and which the Hellenized Christian communities would have translated as *logos*. Furthermore, the opening lines of John are identical with those of the Greek translation of Genesis (the Septuagint), and the content of vss. 1-3 appears to be a "deliberate parallel to the opening chapters of Genesis."[51] Therefore, the writer of the Gospel of John draws upon the Hebraic concept of the Word of God being his creative power and attaches that idea to the early Christian community's assertion that the power of God was in the man Jesus (e.g., Matt. 12:28 and John 3:16-18). In so doing, the writer of John made available to both the Hebraic and the Greek mind the Christian story and proclamation about the man Jesus. Yet, neither the Stoic nor the Gnostic nor the Jew could agree with the notion that the Word had become flesh, or human.[52] Therefore, while using concepts familiar to the Stoics, Gnostics, and the Jewish community in general, John transposes the Christian proclamation into the term *logos*. R. C. Grant sums up well John's special use of the term *logos*:

> As with "Messiah" and *"Logos,"* when it is said of Jesus that he is (the) Messiah or that "the *Logos* became flesh" in him, by and in those statements "Messiah" and *"Logos"* acquire a meaning which, in their totality, they had not carried before: their Christian context is more important for their meaning than their earlier history.[53]

The same could be said of John's use of dualistic categories. In using dualistic motifs (such as light and darkness) known in other Near Eastern contexts (Iran's Zoroastrianism, Jewish apocalyptic, and the Gnostic Hermetica) the Gospel's author used available linguistic channels to convey his ideas to a wide audience, both Greek and non-Greek.

Finally, John's Prologue represents a reinterpretation of the central message of God's presence among men in such a fashion that those raised in a Hellenistic world could understand it.[54] The self-expressed purpose of the whole of John is "that you may believe that Jesus is the Christ, the Son of God, and that believing you may have life in his name" (John 20:31). By using Greek concepts that also had roots in the Hebrew and early Christian traditions, John defends the Christian message against those very traditions from which he borrows terms and concepts. Furthermore, the Prologue defends the person Jesus over against John the Baptist and his disciples, as do other portions of the Gospel of John (e.g., 1:20; 3:28; 4:2; 10:41).[55] As a reflective retelling of the story of Jesus from the point of view of personal religion, John's Prologue offers a creative presentation and defense of the early Christian message.

Buddha's Four Sights

The story of young Gautama's renunciation contains within it an episode that explains why the young prince left his comfortable home to assume the ascetic life. The narrative can be summarized:

> Gautama's father, King Suddhodana, attempted to protect his young son from viewing the ills of the world. He built three castles for Prince Gautama, one for winter, one for spring and autumn, and one for summer. The young prince lived a life of extreme comfort "wholly given over to pleasure."
>
> One day, the young prince decided to go for a ride in a nearby park and told his charioteer to prepare the chariot. The gods in heaven, realizing the time was ripe for the future Buddha to begin his quest, plotted together to make sights of the real world of pain and suffering available to the sheltered prince Gautama.
>
> As the chariot moved along the road to the park, one of the gods took the form of a "decrepit old man, broken-toothed, gray haired, crooked and bent of body, leaning on a staff, and trembling, and showed him to the Future Buddha, but so that only he and the charioteer saw him."
>
> The perplexed prince asked his charioteer who the strange looking man was. The driver responded that the gray haired man was simply old, and that all persons lived toward that same state. Gautama responded, "'Shame on birth, since to everyone that

is born old age must come.' And agitated in heart, he thereupon returned and ascended his palace."

On another day, while the Śākyan prince journeyed toward the park, another god assumed the form of a diseased man. A similar dialogue ensued, with the young prince further disturbed by the sight of painful illness. Yet again, a third trip to the park was halted by a funeral caravan, and the future Buddha was shocked by his first encounter with death. No effort by Suddhodana to cheer up the young prince would work. Plays, dancing girls, music, all failed.

Finally on his fourth trip to the park, the disillusioned Gautama saw a monk with shaven head. When he asked who that man was, he was told, "Sire, this is one who has retired from the world." And the affluent prince "proceeded to sound the praises of retirement from the world. The thought of retiring from the world was a pleasing one to the Future Buddha, . . ."

That night, Prince Siddhartha Gautama left his family and his future throne to search for a peace more durable than the pleasures he had known. Gautama had renounced the desire-filled ways of the world.[56]

According to this story, Prince Gautama renounced the world as a result of the four sights. The shock of seeing in three persons the whole aging process was eased only by the fourth sight, which pointed a way to release from the chain of existence.

Most commentators conclude that the story of the four sights is most likely a late fabrication added to the life-story of Gautama. G. C. Pande gives two reasons for his agreement with this conclusion. In the first place, Pande argues that a young man, even a prince, could not live for twenty-eight years without seeing the aging and dying of persons. A second, contextural reason is that the earliest Pāli traditions (the Nikāyas) do not mention the story of the four sights. The early texts do mention reflection by Gautama on the processes of life, which are "birth, old age, disease, death, sorrow, and corruption." [57] But the same text states very simply Gautama's reason for his renunciation: "Cramped is this household life, the home of dust. Free as air is going forth. Thus seeing, he went forth." It would seem that the early Nikāya traditions describe the future Buddha as a troubled young man who became disgusted with the world when he realized that he, too, was subject to old age, sickness, and death. [58] Furthermore, it is not difficult to see how such a tradition could be developed into story form and added as the conclusive element in Gautama's renunciation of the world. [59] The story of the four sights preserves the two essential thrusts of the earlier tradition: (1) the need to extinguish sensual passions and craving for material luxuries, which tied Gautama to a transitory world, and (2) Gautama's apparent desire to attain an eternal peace. [60] The twofold stress of renunciation and quest is expressed simply by the Buddha near the end of his life.:

> But twenty-nine was I when I renounced
> The world, Subhadda, seeking after the Good.
> For fifty years and one year more, Subhadda,
> Since I went out, a pilgrim have I been
> Through the wide realm of System and of Law—
> Outside of that no victory can be won! [61]

The Anguttara Nikāya relates several episodes that utilize the threefold sights as a reason for renouncing the world and may have been the impetus for the story of the four sights of Prince Siddhartha. The first episode begins when a young man named Hatthaka of nearby Āḷavī asks the Buddha if he is happy. The Buddha answers in the affirmative. The young man asks how the Buddha can be happy sitting on hard ground in the winter with gale winds piercing his thin robes. The Buddha asks Hatthaka if he would be happy living in a luxurious house with a soft bed covered with wool and being waited upon by four wives as servants. The young man answers quickly, he would. Then the Buddha asks if torments born of lust would not arise to bring unhappiness into such a luxurious home. Again the Buddha asks if torments of the flesh (illness) could also not intrude into such a home. Hatthaka answers positively both times. The Buddha says, "Well, my lad, as to those torments [body and mind] . . . that delusion has been abandoned by the Tathāgata. . . . That is why I live happily."[62]

There follows immediately upon the story of Hatthaka, a story by the Buddha on the three messengers of Death (Yama). The story commences with the death of an immoral person who failed to respect his mother, father, and the sages he had met. Dragged before Yama, the Lord of Death, the person-soul was asked if he had not seen the first Messenger of Death. He said he had not. Yama responds,

> What! My good man, have you never seen a human being, . . . eighty or ninety or a hundred years of age, broken down, bent inwards like the rafter of a roof, crooked, staff-propped, and trembling as he goes along,—an ailing [creature] past his prime, with broken teeth, gray-haired or hairless, bald, with wrinkled brow and limbs all blotched and spotted?

The person-soul answered that he had seen such a sight. Yama then responded, "My good man, did it never occur to you as a man of intelligence and fully grown: I too am subject to old age, I have not overpassed old age. Come let me act nobly in deed, word and thought?" Then Yama proceeds to instruct the dead person through questions

about the other two messengers of Death: (1) disease and
(2) swollen, rotting corpses. There ends the story of the
three messengers of Death: old age, disease/illness, and
dead remains.[63]

It seems that the Buddha or his immediate followers
used the same three signs of decay (old age, illness, and
death) in a variety of circumstances to warn others of the
delusion and false happiness attachment to the world
brings. So too the way of the monk was exalted as the
life-style that could lead to cessation of desires that attach
a person to the transitory world. The Buddha, advanced in
age, used the same three reflections on decay to speak of
his renunciation of pride in his youth. One segment of
those reminiscences exposes the pattern:

> Now I too am subject to old age and decay. Were I to see
> another broken down with old age, I might be troubled,
> ashamed and disgusted. That would not be seemly in me.
> Thus, monks, as I considered the matter, all pride in my youth
> deserted me.[64]

The same formula is used by the Buddha to discuss
disease and death. The three signs of decay, therefore, are
viewed as subjects of reflection that can destroy pride and
bring about the detachment from worldly pleasures that
Gautama's renunciation exemplified. The fourth sign, the
wandering monk, is a positive subject of reflection on the
way permanent happiness and calm can be reached.

The story of the four signs of Prince Siddhartha
represents, therefore, a reflective myth that makes plausible the need for renunciation of the world by the young
prince Gautama. The late appearance of the story in the
Pāli traditions suggests that the four-sights story is a
fictional episode that was added to the early life of the
Buddha. The presence of the threefold reflections on
decay in the early traditions does indicate that the

four-sights story is likely a personalization of a reflective incident that did form the basis of the renunciation of Gautama. In traditional Buddhism the four-encounters story is used as a paradigmatic tale of the Buddha that explains why the Buddha renounced the world (reflective myth) and why *all* persons should do the same. Furthermore, the story of the four sights confirms the Buddha's understanding of the world as *duḥkha* and *anitya*. As such, the narrative describes the transience and suffering of the world through the symbols of old age, sickness, and death. Even further, the myth reasons that the way out of *saṃsāra* is the way of renunciation—the way of the monk.

Summary Comments

Most surveys of the world's religious traditions begin with a presentation of the "beliefs" of those traditions. Creation motifs, ethical injunctions, and ritual behavior are included in those accounts. Such a focus, however, may mislead the uninitiated reader into concluding that the beliefs themselves represent the core of a given religious tradition. In this essay it has been argued that reflective formulations often stand as the furthest extension of the personal experience that gave rise to that tradition. Even when they are a part of the domain of personal religiosity, reflective myths and statements constitute the products of thought as applied or related to experiences of a Sacred Power. Consequently, the creation stories of Genesis are primarily an application of faith in the omnipresence and omnipotence of Yahweh, just as the Johannine hymn recasts reflectively the sacred narrative of God's self-sacrifice on behalf of all people. Such stories are the last to come into a tradition, not the first, and should be studied in their proper order.

Moreover, in the environs of social religion, reflective formulations have the formidable task of providing plausibility for or legitimation of the claims of a particular religious practice or belief. For example, the story of the four visions provides the social legitimation for the Buddha's (and all later monks') renunciation of the world. Religious reflections, therefore, are often the most visible aspects to outsiders of a religious tradition as they explain, defend, and make plausible the practices and perspectives not shared by other competing social realities. I do not intend to suggest that their posterior position in the chronology and experience of a religious tradition renders them unimportant. On the contrary, because most persons are not members of a founding generation, socialization and legitimation are usually the first avenues to religious awareness for most persons. Therefore, the ability of religious reflection to provide plausible answers for the new initiate or the faltering member may determine the very future (or lack of it) for a religious tradition. For example, debates continue to rage between evolutionists and defenders of the Genesis myths, as a battle between the scientific reality and the religious reality with their different assumptions and "truths." And converts are often won or lost based on the plausibility of theological conclusions.

Religious reflection, therefore, stands in the crucial position of having to debate other realities on *their* battlegrounds, devoid of assumptions of Sacred Power. In the end, however, it would seem that such deliberative arguments and defenses are basically the rationalizations for conclusions already reached experientially. To initiate a study of any religious tradition with beliefs, creeds, and dogmas, then, is to begin at the end.

Conclusion:
Two Kinds of Swimmers

There remain master shipbuilders who claim they can teach others how to sail or to swim to the forgotten paradise. Many persons have learned the mechanics of sailing and swimming through charts and books and their master's words, yet have never themselves swum in the open sea. Others have swum far out into uncharted waters and have told of their adventures in the vivid language of the sage and the prophet. Both groups are still ridiculed as one by the revolutionaries, who have grown in numbers and confidence. The revolutionaries still taunt, "If there is any validity in ships and swimming show us ships that have made the journey and swimmers who have come back!" Such a challenge makes the swimmers who have yet to experience the uncharted and mysterious waters very uneasy. They too have wished for some kind of proof of the benefits of their hard-earned skills and hours of committed service. However, those who have swum in the calm sea tell a story of their life in the primordial ocean, or, like the Buddha, maintain a serene silence. The revolutionaries are now armed with reason refined into disciplines known as philosophy, psychology, and sociology. Such weapons have demolished the faith of some of the swimmers whose experience is limited to the words of the masters and the rituals of the collectivity. However, those who have thrilled to the touch of the sea are unmoved by the logic of the revolutionaries, who are judged to be limited by their lack of experiences beyond the island of mortals.

In this essay, I have tried to take seriously two basic dimensions of human development: social conditioning and personal experience. To be sure, those who adopt a sociological interpretation of religious behavior and thought also account for personal experiences as socially governed sensations. What I have done in my analysis is to recognize the *possibility* of religious experience arising from sources other than society or "ripe" psychological moods and circumstances. It is quite clear that social processes (especially language) shape the reception and expression of all human experience. It does not follow, however, that social processes control completely all that a person may experience or become. What I have presented in my notion of two sacred worlds, then, is an interpretation of religious experience (and its conse-quences) that does not prejudge the validity or source of those experiences which have given rise to religious traditions throughout the world—regardless of time or culture.

While two sacred worlds represent two distinct existen-tial realms, these two religious worlds may, and most often do, overlap and interrelate. One analytical benefit of recognizing these distinctive modes of experience is to understand more clearly the relationship and various functions of disparate myths, rituals, and ethical injunc-tions. For example, one might conclude from such a twofold perspective of the religious life that Hebrew dietary laws, Christian dress codes, and Buddhist admoni-tions concerning the eremitic life have different value and functions for the personally religious "holy person" than they have for the socialized laity. But more important, we may recognize that ethical injunctions in any religious tradition reflect social needs and values but also bear the stamp of the core impulse of each tradition, which gives those ethics their particular meaning and interpretation. Consequently, the Hebrew commandment of non-killing did not extend to treatment of the enemies of the Hebrew people or even to criminals among the Hebrews themselves. On the other hand, the Buddhist notion of non-injury *(ahimsa)* applied much more broadly to all worldly beings, human and animal. Similar differences in value and function apply to the myths, rituals, and ethics of all religious traditions.

What has been presented in this study as a twofold structure of experience is, in its empirical situation, a complex human and social phenomenon. For example, a personal religion may arise from an initial experience that gives rise to institutional objectification, as a codifying reality within an already accepted social religion, or as a phenomenon wholly separate from any particular institutionalized religious tradition. Likewise, social religion is the product of social forces broader in scope than those associated only with institutional religion. Finally, the very determination of who is personally or socially religious is finally known only by the person who claims a particular faith stance. To wit, only those who are reciting the Lord's Prayer or the Buddhist *dhamma* know the strength and influence those words have for them. Still, the actions of all persons, religious or not, give no small insight into the basic ground upon which they truly stand. Consequently, if a basic twofold distinction of foundation (*i.e.,* religious experience vs. socialization) does exist, then it behooves investigators of religious phenomena to uncover both dimensions of religious awareness in whatever religious traditions they study. It would appear, therefore, that the twofold analysis of religious traditions also bears some consequence for the way in which religious traditions should be studied.

In the methodological sphere it should be clear from my analysis of three religious traditions what questions I use to investigate religious phenomena. However, the evidence is not always available to ascertain what it was that persons of a particular religious community stressed in their behavior or what social factors were present as influences that affected the original expression of ritual, ethical, or theological ideas. Furthermore, not every religious tradition has written religious texts, a known religious founder, or a persistent ritual history. Still, the attempt to relate certain central rituals and ethics to corresponding core myths can serve to uncover key experiences that help to explain other, less central practices and myths. That is, we may come to know why it is that not all myths, rituals, and ethical commands enjoy an equal status in any given religious tradition's theory or practice.

Finally, when opportunities occur for one to observe living religious traditions (familiar or foreign) in their social setting, questions of social needs, functions, and perceptions must be balanced with their personal counterparts. Consequently, whether layperson or scholar, we should be slow to apply only the logic of the revolutionaries without at least first listening to the stories of the swimmers. And even more important, we must not confuse the stories of those who have learned only indirectly from charts and books with the tales of the sages who have tested the water and have swum in the mysterious sea. It has been pointed out to most laypersons and scholars that two options for living are represented by the sacred and profane modes of existence. It is my hope that this essay has demonstrated the less obvious, but equally crucial, recognition that there are, in fact, two modes of awareness of any sacred reality—that is, two sacred worlds in which persons of any faith can live.

NOTES

Introduction

1. *The Sufis* (Garden City, N.Y.: Doubleday, 1964), pp. 1-10.
2. *The Rites of Passage*, trans. Monika B. Vizedom and Gabrielle L. Caffee (Chicago: University of Chicago Press, 1960), pp. 20, 89, *passim*.
3. The Elementary Forms of the Religious Life, trans. Joseph Ward Swain (New York: The Free Press, 1965).
4. Trans. Willard R. Trask (Torch books; New York: Harper, 1961), p. 14. See also, Rudolf Otto, *The Idea of the Holy*, trans. John W. Harvey (New York: Oxford University Press, 1958).
5. Michael Novak, *Ascent of the Mountain, Flight of the Dove* (New York: Harper, 1971), p. 28.
6. *Ibid.*, p. 32.

Chapter 1. The Religion of Personal Experience

1. *The Politics of Experience* (New York: Ballantine Books, 1967), p. 137.
2. *Ascent of the Mountain*, p. 28.
3. *The Varieties of Religious Experience: A Study in Human Nature* (New York: Collier Books, 1961), pp. 24, 25. Abraham Maslow, a contemporary psychologist, agrees as he says, "The very beginning, the intrinsic core, the essence, the universal nucleus of every known high religion . . . has been the private, lonely, personal illumination, revelation, or ecstasy of some acutely sensitive prophet or seer." In *Religions, Values, and Peak-Experiences* (Columbus: Ohio State University Press, 1964), p. 19.
4. *Varieties*, p. 41. For full description, see pp. 39-58.
5. *Ibid.*, p. 42. James discusses theology as solely an institutional activity; I do not. See ch. 5, "Religious Reflection and World Construction."
6. John M. Moore, *Theories of Religious Experience* (New York: Round Table Press, 1938), p. 6.
7. Maslow, *Religions, Values, Peak-Experiences*, p. xii.

8. Huston Smith, "Do Drugs Have Religious Import?" in *LSD: The Consciousness Expanding Drug*, ed. David Soloman (Medallion Books; New York: Berkley, 1964), p. 160.
9. *Varieties*, pp. 299-300.
10. In ch. 3 I discuss briefly the nature of symbols and symbolic language. To do justice to the vast literature on this subject more space would be needed than is available in this study.
11. The following summary is taken from Joachim Wach, *The Comparative Study of Religions* (New York: Columbia University Press, 1958), pp. 30-37.
12. *The Idea of the Holy*, pp. 12-30.
13. Compare Gordon Allport's notion of "gradual awakening" in *The Individual and His Religion* (New York: Macmillan, 1950), p. 34.
14. Horace Bushnell, *Christian Nurture* (New Haven: Yale University Press, 1888), pp. 3-4.
15. *Life and Letters of Horace Bushnell*, ed. Mary Bushnell Cheney (New York: Harper, 1880), p. 192.
16. Helmut Ringgren, *Israelite Religion*, trans. David E. Green (Philadelphia: Fortress Press, 1966), pp. 39-41.
17. *Ibid.*, pp. 17-27.
18. *Ibid.*, p. 20.
19. The main source for the following analysis is the Hebrew scripture called the Torah, the first five books of the Old Testament. Actually, the Torah represents not one source, but several. By literary and contextual criticism, scholars have identified at least four different oral traditions, which are interwoven into a whole so that the Torah is presented as the work of one author, Moses. These oral traditions are commonly identified as J (a Yahwist tradition going back to the ninth or tenth century B.C.); E (a tradition using Elohim for the deity's name and reaching back to the eighth century B.C.); D (the Deuteronomic tradition, originating in the mid-seventh century B.C.); and P (a second Elohist tradition, evidencing priestly concerns and dating from the fifth century B.C.). While these dates are approximate and the traditions are not fully delineated, the basic point is that the Hebrew scriptures represent a blending of various oral traditions and thereby a blending of various theological and ethical positions. For our consideration it is important to note that the book of Exodus represents an intertwining of the J, E, and P traditions. Without burdening the reader with tedious and continual references to the tradition a particular text represents, I shall try to be faithful to the dating of sources by referring to "early" and "late" or "beginning" and "later" features of Yahwist religion.
20. *History of Israelite Religion*, trans. David E. Green (Nashville: Abingdon Press, 1972), p. 29.
21. *Ibid.*, pp. 70-74.
22. Scholars have reached various conclusions regarding the pre-

Hebrew history of the Yahweh cult. For example, Ringgren calls Yahweh a Kenite god in *Israelite Religion*, p. 35, and Fohrer identifies Yahweh as a Midianite deity in *History of Israelite Religion*, p. 75.

23. Fohrer, *History of Israelite Religion*, p. 77.

24. *Primitive Christianity: In Its Contemporary Setting*, trans. R. H. Fuller (New York: World, 1956), p. 187.

25. For a summary treatment of the cultural background of Jesus' day, see: William Foxwell Albright, *From the Stone Age to Christianity* (Anchor Books; Garden City, N.Y.: Doubleday, 1957), pp. 334-80; and Gunther Bornkamm, *Jesus of Nazareth* (New York: Harper, 1960), pp. 27-52. For longer treatments of Hellenistic backgrounds to the early Christian times, see: Frederick C. Grant, *Roman Hellenism and the New Testament* (New York: Scribner's, 1962); and Arthur Darby Nock, *Early Gentile Christianity and Its Hellenistic Background* (Torchbooks; New York: Harper, 1964). For a rehearsal of Jewish traditions that served as a backdrop for early Christianity, see: Frederick C. Grant, *Ancient Judaism and the New Testament* (New York: Macmillan, 1959); and W. D. Davies, *Christian Origins and Judaism* (London: Darton, Longman & Todd, 1962).

26. See "Jesus as Son of Man," ch. 2; also M. Rist, "Apocalypticism" in *The Interpreter's Dictionary of the Bible* (Nashville: Abingdon Press, 1962), I, 157-61.

27. For example, see "The Christian Logos or Word," in ch. 5. Rudolph Bultmann goes so far as to postulate possible influence from the Greek mystery religions (see *Primitive Christianity*, pp. 156-61).

28. *The Founder of Christianity* (New York: Macmillan, 1970), p. 26.

29. *Jesus of Nazareth*, p. 16.

30. *Founder of Christianity*, pp. 37-52.

31. Bornkamm, *Jesus of Nazareth*, pp. 53-55.

32. Though it should be understood that Jesus' view of himself and that of the disciples may well have coincided.

33. This is Laing's point when he says that experience comes before belief: *Politics of Experience*, p. 141. While Douglas A. Fox's book *Mystery and Meaning: Personal Logic and the Language of Religion* (Philadelphia: Westminster Press, 1975) was published only after this manuscript was already on the publisher's desk, it is not insignificant that Fox develops a model (pp. 25-36) similar to my own as he asserts, "The Generating Experience of Christianity is the awakening to the 'Christhood' of Jesus of Nazareth" (p. 106).

34. *Founder of Christianity*, p. 28.

35. See *Primitive Christianity*, pp. 175-79 and *Theology of the New Testament* (New York: Scribner's, 1951), I, 292-314, where Bultmann treats the death *and* resurrection as one event.

36. *Jesus of Nazareth*, p. 180.

37. *Ibid.*, pp. 180-81.

38. *Politics of Experience*, p. 144.
39. *Jesus of Nazareth*, p. 16.
40. *Ibid.*, p. 186.
41. Edward J. Thomas, *The Life of the Buddha* (London: Routledge & Kegan Paul, 1927), p. 27; Gobind Chandra Pande, *Studies in the Origins of Buddhism* (Allahabad, India: University of Allahabad, 1957), pp. 371-72; Richard Henry Drummond, *Gautama the Buddha* (Grand Rapids: Eerdmans, 1974), p. 27.
42. Trevor Ling, *The Buddha* (London: Temple Smith, 1973), pp. 37-39.
43. *Ibid.*, p. 45.
44. See: Arthur Berriedale Keith, *The Religion and Philosophy of the Veda and Upanishads*, Harvard Oriental Series, Vols. 31 and 32 (Cambridge: Harvard University Press, 1925).
45. Pande, *Origins of Buddhism*, p. 281.
46. For discussion of the śramaṇa movements in ancient and classical India, see: Nalinaksha Dutt, *Early Monastic Buddhism* (Calcutta: Oriental Book Agency, 1960), pp. 27-76; and Pande, *Origins of Buddhism*, pp. 251-61 and 326-68.
47. See, e.g.: Bṛihadāraṇyaka Upanishad 1.1, 2 in Robert Ernest Hume, *The Thirteen Principle Upanishads* (paperback; Oxford: Oxford University Press, 1971), pp. 73-74; and Muṇḍaka Upanishad 1. 2 in Hume, *Upanishads* pp. 367-69.
48. Sir Monier Monier-Williams, *A Sanskrit-English Dictionary* (Oxford: Clarendon Press, 1899), p. 1119.
49. Maitri Upanishad 1.3, 4 in Hume, *Upanishads*, p. 413.
50. Heinrich Zimmer, *Myths and Symbols in Indian Art and Civilization*, ed. Joseph Campbell (New York: Pantheon Books, 1946), pp. 3-11.
51. Bṛihadāraṇyaka Upanishad 4. 4. 5; Hume, *Upanishads*, p. 140.
52. 11.1, 2; Hume, *Upanishads*, pp. 281-82.
53. For a summary of several basic groupings of *dharma* see: Sarvepalli Radhakrishnan and Charles A. Moore, *A Source Book in Indian Philosophy* (Princeton: Princeton University Press, 1957), pp. 172-92.
54. Rig Veda X. 136, trans. Ralph T. H. Griffith, *The Hymns of the Rigveda* (Bernaras: E. J. Lazarus and Co., 1892), IV, 377-378. Compare Atharva Veda VII. 1-5, trans. William Dwight Whitney, *Atharva-Veda-Saṁhita*, Harvard Oriental Series (Cambridge: Harvard University Press, 1905), VII, 388-92.
55. *Ibid.*
56. Monier-Williams, *Sanskrit-English Dictionary*, p. 1043.
57. *Origins of Buddhism*, p. 259.
58. Monier-Williams, *Sanskrit-English Dictionary*, p. 1096.
59. Pande, *Origins of Buddhism*, p. 328.
60. *Ibid.*, p. 260.
61. *Ibid.*

62. Thomas, *Life of the Buddha*, p. xix.
63. The three collections of Pāli Canon are (1) the Sutta Piṭaka ("Basket of Verses"), (2) the Vinaya Piṭaka ("Basket of Moral Teachings"), and (3) the Abhidhamma Piṭaka ("Basket of Higher Teachings"). For a full discussion of the nature, summary, content, and the dating of the texts of the Pāli Tripiṭaka see Maurice Winternitz, *A History of Indian Literatures*, Vol. II, trans. S. Ketkar and H. Kohn (New York: Russell & Russell, 1933), pp. 1-423. G. C. Pande makes a detailed attempt to untangle the various threads of tradition woven together in the three Piṭakas in his *Origins of Buddhism*, pp. 1-256. Edward J. Thomas lists in an annotated outline the texts included in the Pāli Canon by the fifth century A.D. in *Life of the Buddha*, pp. 257-77.
64. *Gautama the Buddha*, p. 26. For an old but still valuable description of the Pāli accounts of Gautama Buddha's life, see: A. C. A. Foucher, *The Life of the Buddha, According to the Ancient Text and Monuments of India*, trans. Simone B. Boas (Middletown, Conn.: Wesleyan University Press, 1963); also, Tibetan translations of the *Vinaya* traditions have been rendered into English by W. W. Rockhill, *The Life of the Buddha* (London: Truebner, 1884); Buddhist Sanskrit biographies of the Buddha include the Buddhacarita ("Adventures of the Buddha") by Aśvaghoṣa and the Lalitavistara ("The Extended Sports" of the Buddha), both of which were compiled approximately at the end of the first century A.D. A third Sanskrit text, which contains traditions reaching back to Aśoka's time (third century B.C.) but was not fully compiled until the third or fourth century A.D., is called the Mahāvastu ("The Great Story"). The Mahāvastu is attached to the *Vinaya* of an early schismatic school and nearly parallels verbatim whole sections of the Mahāvagga of the Pāli Vinaya Piṭaka. The Mahāvastu is a collection of Buddhist legends and tales related to the many lives of the Buddha. Two Singhalese chronicles that tell of Buddha's journeys to Ceylon are the Dīpavaṃsa ("Island Chronicle") and the Mahāvaṃsa ("Great Chronicle")—these chronicles belong to the fourth and fifth centuries A.D. respectively. In the fifth century A.D., the famous translator and commentator Buddhaghosa translated from Singhalese back into Pāli the Nidānakathā ("The Treasured Story"), which serves as the introductory biography of the Buddha to the famous Jatakas ("Birth Tales") of the Buddha.
65. Walpola Sri Rahula, *What the Buddha Taught* (Bedford, England: Gordon Fraser, 1967), pp. 1-15.
66. This view of the Buddha was not shared, even in the earliest times, by most laymen and several monastic sects. For example, see Edward Conze, *Buddhism: Its Essence and Development* (Torchbooks; New York: Harper, 1959), pp. 34-40 and 145 ff.
67. Secondary sources used are Thomas, *Life of the Buddha*, pp. 26-96; Pande, *Origins of Buddhism*, pp. 369-94; and Drummond,

Gautama the Buddha, pp. 25-83.

68. Such a pattern had been followed by young men previously in the Ganges culture and would become the idealized way in Buddhism, Jainism, and other "heretical" movements of that era.
69. Drummond, *Gautama the Buddha,* p. 35.
70. The two teachers apparently taught six or seven stages of mental awareness, the highest of which, for Gautama, fell short of supreme enlightenment.
71. This section of the Dīgha Nikāya comprises the famous Mahā-Satipaṭṭhāna-Sutta ("The Great Foundations of Mindfulness"), which will be explored more fully in ch. 3 under "Buddhist Meditation."
72. *Middle Length Sayings,* trans. I. B. Horner (London: Luzac & Company, 1967), I, 27-29.
73. *The Dialogues of the Buddha* I, trans. T. W. Rhys Davids. (Vol. I: *Sacred Books of the Buddhists,* ed. T. W. Rhys Davids [London: Oxford University Press, 1895–1951], p. 26 [Dīgha Nikāya I. 12]. Hereafter, this series will be cited as *Sacred Books.*)
74. Drummond, *Gautama the Buddha,* pp. 38-44, and G. C. Pande, *Origins of Buddhism,* pp. 379-80.
75. Drummond, *Gautama the Buddha,* pp. 113-27; G. C. Pande, *Origins of Buddhism,* pp. 443-510; Thomas, *Life of the Buddha,* pp. 81-88.
76. *The Book of the Kindred Sayings* I, trans. C. A. F. Rhys Davids. (Vol. VII: Translation Series of the Pali Text Society, ed. C. A. F. Rhys Davids [London: Luzac & Company, 1913–36], pp. 173-74 [Saṁyutta-Nikāya I. 138]. Hereafter this series will be cited as *Translation Series.)* The interpretation of Buddha's decision to teach others his path as a compassionate act becomes formulated as an obligation of the liberated monk. See further, *Dialogues of the Buddha* I, (*Sacred Books,* V, 27 [Majjhima Nikāya I. 38]).
77. Pande, *Origins of Buddhism,* p. 394.

Chapter 2. The Religion of Social Experience

1. *The Elementary Forms of the Religious Life,* p. 466.
2. *The Social Construction of Reality* (Anchor Books; New York: Doubleday, 1967), pp. 1, 15.
3. *Ibid.,* pp. 15-16.
4. *Ibid.,* p. 21.
5. Paraphrasing Max Scheler as quoted in *ibid.,* p. 8.
6. I have been guided in my analysis of social religion by the work of Berger and Luckmann in their joint work *The Social Construction of Reality,* plus Berger's two recent books, *The Sacred Canopy: Elements of a Sociological Theory of Religion* (Anchor Books; New York: Doubleday, 1969) and *A Rumor of Angels: Modern Society and the Rediscovery of the Supernatural* (Anchor Books, 1970).
7. Berger's terminology, *Sacred Canopy,* p. 4.

8. Berger and Luckmann, *Social Construction*, p. 139.
9. *Ibid.*, p. 131.
10. *Ibid.*, pp. 130-38.
11. *Ibid.*, p. 53.
12. *Religions, Values, and Peak-Experiences*, p. 34.
13. *Ritual Process* (Chicago: Aldine Publishing Co., 1969), pp. 94-130.
14. *Ibid.*, p. 133.
15. *Ibid.*, p. 188. The basic modification here of most social theories of institutionalization is the recognition of the whole person—emotions and intellect.
16. *Ibid.*, p. 203. Such an analysis becomes most fruitful in a discussion of ritual with its social and personal implications, as later discussions will reveal.
17. See ch. 1, cumulative, pp. 26-29.
18. Evidence the number of students who argue their religion.
19. *Varieties*, p. 42.
20. See Maslow, *Religions, Values, and Peak-Experiences*, pp. 20-24.
21. *Ibid.*, p. 28.
22. *Ibid.*, p. 24.
23. *Ibid.*, pp. 30-31.
24. Novak, *Ascent of the Mountain*, p. 156.
25. *Politics of Experience*, pp. 57-76.
26. Cf. Maslow, *Religions, Values, and Peak-Experiences*, p. 20.
27. *Israelite Religion*, pp. 21-23.
28. *Ibid.*, p. 42.
29. P. A. H. DeBoer, *Fatherhood and Motherhood in Israelite and Judean Piety* (Leiden: E. S. Brill, 1974), pp. 26, 30.
30. See I Enoch in C. K. Barrett, ed., *The New Testament Background: Selected Documents* (Torchbooks; New York: Harper, 1961), pp. 252-55.
31. *Ibid.*, pp. 235-37. Perhaps Bultmann's understanding of "Son of man" as simply a circuitous Greek way of translating the Aramaic word for "man" is of value here. Rudolph Bultmann, *Primitive Christianity*, p. 217, n 44.
32. For the debate over Jesus' messianic consciousness, see Albright, *From the Stone Age*, p. 395.
33. Compare I En. 69:26.
34. *Jesus of Nazareth*, p. 178.
35. *Saṅgha* literally means "assemblage or collection"; see Monier-Williams, *Sanskrit-English Dictionary*, p. 1129.
36. N. Dutt, *Monastic Buddhism*, p. 73, and Sukumar Dutt, *Buddhist Monks and Monasteries of India* (London: Allen Unwin, 1962), p. 86.
37. Ling, *The Buddha*, p. 51.
38. S. Dutt, *Buddhist Monks*, p. 86.
39. N. Dutt, *Monastic Buddhism*, p. 74.
40. *Ibid.*

41. "Last Days of the Buddha," *The Wheel Publication*, No. 67-69 (Kandy, Ceylon: Buddhist Publication Society, 1964), p. 27 (Dīgha Nikāya II. 100). This is a more recent translation of the "Mahāparinibbāna Sutta," which can also be found in *Dialogues of the Buddha* II (*Sacred Books*, III, 78-191).
42. "Last Days," *Wheel*, p. 73 (Dīgha Nikāya II. 154.)
43. *Ibid.*, p. 27 (Dīgha Nikāya II. 100).
44. Ling, *The Buddha*, pp. 131-33.
45. S. Dutt, *The Buddha and Five After Centuries* (London: Luzac & Company, 1957), p. 61. A comparable notion in Western Christianity is of the "catholic" or universal church.
46. "Last Days," *Wheel*, pp. 7-8 (Dīgha Nikāya II. 80).
47. *Monastic Buddhism*, p. 74.
48. Kenneth K. S. Chen, *Buddhism: The Light of Asia* (New York: Barron's Educational Series, 1968), p. 87.
49. *Ibid.*, p. 88.
50. *Ibid.*, p. 86.
51. *Ibid.*, pp. 94-98. For a recital of the Rules of the Saṅgha (Pāli: Pāttimokkha) see *Vinaya Texts* I, trans. T. W. Rhys Davids and Hermann Oldenberg. [Vol. XIII: *Sacred Books of the East* [Oxford: Claredon Press, 1881], pp. 1-69. Hereafter *SBE*.)
52. *Vinaya Texts* I (*SBE*, XIII, 112 [Mahāvagga I. 11. 1]).
53. For a discussion of the two levels of dharma (ideal and actual practice) as well as a treatment of lay-monk interaction, see Frank Reynolds, "The Two Wheels of Dhamma: A Study of Early Buddhism," in *The Two Wheels of Dhamma*, ed. Bardwell L. Smith (Chambersburg, Pa.: American Academy of Religion, 1972), pp. 6-30. For lay Buddhism and its life and interaction with the monkish community see: S. Dutt, *Five After Centuries*, pp. 143-212; and N. Dutt, *Monastic Buddhism*, pp. 169-94.
54. S. Dutt, *Buddhist Monks*, pp. 53-97.
55. Thomas, *Life of the Buddha*, pp. 165-72.

Chapter 3. Myth and Ritual:
Expression and Habitualization

1. I have chosen "founded" or "revealed" religious traditions to exemplify my interpretation of the two realms of personal and social religion because these traditions most lucidly reveal both sacred worlds. I do not mean to imply, however, that such a bifold descriptive distinction would not pertain to so-called primitive or nature-oriented religious traditions, or to any other religious tradition that had no remembered founder. The data are more difficult to sort out in most tribal or nonliterate cultures, owing to a lack of historical and textual information, but the twofold distinction I make here would seem to apply to all types of religious traditions, including tribal ones.
2. For example, see Lord Raglan, "Myth and Ritual," *Myth: A*

Symposium, ed. Thomas A. Sebeok (Bloomington: Indiana University Press, 1958), pp. 76-83.

3. I do not rule out occurrences of myths arising devoid of corresponding rituals. Nor do I find it unusual for a ritual older than a myth to be adapted to fit that myth. And finally, some rituals clearly serve as the basis for their mythological explanation. Therefore, core myths and rituals are a special species that are central to a religious tradition, and yet their interdependent relationship is not determinative for all other myths and rituals in that tradition.

4. For a sketchy background of some of the current myth theories and theorists, see Percy Cohen, "Theories of Myth," *Man: The Journal of the Royal Anthropological Institute,* Sept., 1969, pp. 337-53; and Dorothy Emmet, "Religion and the Social Anthropology of Religion: III. Myth," *Theoria to Theory,* 1969, pp. 42-55. Special mention should be made of the work of Claude Levi-Strauss, a French anthropologist, whose "structural" approach has been adopted widely as a significant breakthrough in analyzing the nonsemantic logic of myths. See Levi-Strauss, "The Structural Study of Myth," *Structural Anthropology* (Anchor Books; New York: Doubleday, 1967), pp. 202-28, and Edmund Leach, *Claude Levi-Strauss* (New York: Viking, 1970).

5. "The Effectiveness of Symbols," *Structural Anthropology,* pp. 181-201.

6. *Ibid.,* p. 185.

7. *Ibid.,* p. 187.

8. *Ibid.,* pp. 180-81, 188-89.

9. *Ibid.,* p. 190.

10. *Ibid.,* p. 182.

11. While symbols are used in various secular contexts, from poetry to politics, I intend to focus primarily on those symbols understood in a strictly religious sense, *i.e.,* symbols that point to a sacred dimension of reality.

12. "The Symbol Gives Rise to Thought," *Ways of Understanding Religion,* ed. Walter H. Capps (New York: Macmillan, 1972), p. 315.

13. *Ibid.,* p. 316.

14. I follow the lead of Ricoeur, Mircea Eliade, and Percy Cohen in stressing the narrative quality and value of myth. Cohen, for example, concludes that myth "anchors the present in the past," in *Man,* p. 349.

15. For example, see Levi-Strauss, "Structural Study of Myth."

16. Cohen, *Man,* pp. 349-53.

17. Compare Eliade, *Sacred and Profane,* p. 95.

18. A saying popular in rural Ohio, where I was reared, was, "A myth is a story you believe even when you know it isn't true." Cohen's summary runs in the same vein for common usage of the term "myth." He says, "In popular usage the term 'myth' is almost

195

always intended pejoratively: here, my beliefs are strong conviction, yours a dogma, his a myth. Myths, on this view, are erroneous
beliefs clung to against all evidence" (*Man*, p. 337). Fallacy and
fiction are synonyms for this use of myth, and people with
"common sense" (i.e., those who are socialized to believe what
everybody else does) know that myths only fantasize about what
science will soon explain. Clearly, my understanding of myth is
less concerned with epistemological concerns as the place to begin.
Instead, I find it more useful to describe the nature and function of
myth and to leave to others the philosophical and empirical value
judgments that arise from plausibility structures not unlike that of
religion (i.e., experience). Therefore, I find the question of truth or
falsity of myths a matter of experiential opposition as much as
demonstrable logic. Consequently, I reject as too simplistic any
notions of myth that have as their descriptive base an assumption
that all myths are fictitious.

19. Compare Eliade, *Sacred and Profane*, pp. 110-13, and Henri
    Frankfort, "The Emanicipation of Thought from Myth," *Before
    Philosophy* (Baltimore: Penguin Books, 1949), pp. 237-63.
20. *Theology of the New Testament*, I and II.
21. See Berger's argument on different grounds in *Rumor of Angels*,
    pp. 39-40.
22. Much of what follows in my analysis draws its impetus from
    Eliade's *Myth and Reality* (New York: Harper, 1963), pp. 1-20.
23. Eliade ties this "journey back" to archaic time and moments of
    creation. I would make a sharp distinction between myths of
    creation and myths that point to the origin of the cult. The former is
    of the class of reflective myths, while the latter may be expressive
    of experiential events and therefore of a different order altogether.
24. Victor W. Turner, *Ritual Process*, p. 6.
25. Even when the ritual exists prior to the events related in a core
    myth, the adopted ritual is reinterpreted in light of the younger
    myth. The Passover meal and festival is such an example.
26. *Ascent of the Mountain*, p. 109.
27. *Ibid.*, p. 93. Compare Maslow, *Religions, Values, and Peak-
    Experiences*, p. 35.
28. *Rites of Passage*, p. 21. Also Turner, *Ritual Process*, p. 94.
29. *Ritual Process*, pp. 94-165.
30. *Ibid.*, p. 106.
31. *Ibid.*, pp. 132-33.
32. *Ibid.*, pp. 96-97.
33. See "Pentecostal Experience," in *Exploring Religious Meaning*, ed.
    Robert C. Mont *et al.* (Englewood Cliffs, N. J.: Prentice-Hall, 1973),
    pp. 55-57.
34. *Rites of Passage*, p. 29.
35. *Introduction to the Old Testament* (New York: Macmillan, 1971), p.
    118. H. H. Rowley, in a more general way, emphasizes the role of

the Exodus experience when he states, "Israel's faith was based not on speculation, but on experience," in *Worship in Ancient Israel* (London: S.P.C.K., 1967), p. 38.
36. Rowley, *Worship in Ancient Israel*, pp. 40-45.
37. Compare the more developed form of this injunction in Deut. 16:1-17.
38. S. H. Hooke argues that the Passover festival was a New Year's feast in *The Origins of Early Semitic Ritual* (London: Oxford University Press, 1938), pp. 10ff.
39. My own retelling of the verses in Exod. 12:1-20.
40. For other cultic sacrifices see H. H. Rowley's or H. Ringgren's summary descriptions.
41. *History of Israelite Religion*, p. 40.
42. *Worship in Ancient Israel*, p. 47.
43. *Ibid.*, pp. 47-48. See also Walter Harrelson, *From Fertility Cult to Worship* (Anchor Books; Garden City, N.Y.: Doubleday, 1970), pp. 18-19.
44. *Worship in Ancient Israel*, p. 3.
45. *Ibid.*, p. 50.
46. Trans. W. D. Halls (Chicago: University of Chicago Press, 1964).
47. *Ibid.*, p. 97. It is in ritual examples such as this that the ritual theory of Victor Turner seems most clearly to apply—especially when viewed as three phases of religious experience.
48. Fohrer, *History of Israelite Religion*, p. 83.
49. I realize that such a statement runs directly counter to Bornkamm's assertion: "The gospels are the rejection of myth. ... They are given once and for all the function of interpreting the history of Jesus as the history of God with the world," in *Jesus of Nazareth*, p. 23. I would simply observe that "history" is used in a significantly altered sense by Bornkamm, since God, by definition and conception, is a Sacred Power beyond the realm of profane matter and events. To the extent that the story of Jesus ceases to be the story of a human being and becomes the story of God's presence in a historical person, the story of Jesus is a myth (i.e., a story of the Sacred's relationship to the profane world and to mankind).
50. E. O. James places the sacraments of Christianity in the universal context of sacrifice and sacrament in all the world's religious traditions and says, "They have arisen as a result of man's attempt to establish and maintain right relations with the spiritual powers ... and to secure protection from the forces of evil," in *Sacrifice and Sacrament* (London: Thames and Hudson, 1962), p. 11. My treatment of the sacraments will indicate how such phenomenological generalizations increase in value when the specific historical understanding and application within each tradition are taken into account.
51. *Baptism in the New Testament*, trans. J. K. S. Reid, Studies in

Biblical Theology, No. 1 (London: SCM Press, 1950), p. 11.
52. *Ibid.*, pp. 14-15.
53. *Ibid.*, pp. 19-22.
54. Oscar Cullman, *Early Christian Worship*, trans. A. Steward Todd and James B. Torrance, Studies in Biblical Theology, No. 10 (London: SCM Press, 1953), p. 19.
55. *Ibid.*, pp. 14-15.
56. *Ibid.*, p. 15.
57. *Ibid.*, pp. 17-18.
58. *Ibid.*, p. 11. Cullman says that the term "Sunday" arose later as a designation used by those who identified the dead and risen Jesus with a dying and rising sun god (p. 12). Compare E. O. James, *Sacrifice and Sacrament*, pp. 198-208.
59. Cullman, *Early Christian Worship*, p. 29.
60. E. O. James, in *Sacrifice and Sacrament*, pp. 206-7, describes the move from *agape* or love feast to eucharistic ritual.
61. *Early Christian Worship*, pp. 20-21.
62. *Sacrifice and Sacrament*, p. 251.
63. *Buddhism*, p. 95.
64. *The Dialogues of the Buddha* II (*Sacred Books*, III, 343-45 [Dīgha Nikāya XXII. 311-13]). See also Rahula, *What the Buddha Taught*.
65. Chen, *Light of Asia*, p. 33, and Rahula, *What the Buddha Taught*, p. 47.
66. *The Dialogues of the Buddha* II (*Sacred Books*, III, 108 [Dīgha Nikāya II. 100]).
67. *The Heart of Buddhist Meditation* (New York: Samuel Weiser, 1962), pp. 23-24.
68. *Dialogue of the Buddha* II (*Sacred Books*, III, 327 [Dīgha Nikāya XXII. 290; see also Majjhima Nikāya X]).
69. Drummond, *Gautama the Buddha*, pp. 35-36.
70. Mircea Eliade, *Patanjali and Yoga*, trans. Charles Lam Markmann (New York: Funk & Wagnalls, 1969), pp. 160-61; see also Śvetāśvatara Upaniṣad 2. 8-15 in Hume, *Upanishads*, pp. 398-99.
71. *Dialogues of the Buddha* II (*Sacred Books*, III, 328 [Dīgha Nikāya XXII. 291]). Compare an early reference to yoga in the Svetāśvatara Upaniṣad 2. 8-15 in Hume, *Upanishads*, pp. 398-99.
72. Nyanaponika, *Buddhist Meditation*, p. 61.
73. *The Dialogues of the Buddha* II (*Sacred Books*, III, 328 [Dīgha Nikāya XXII. 291]).
74. *Ibid.*, pp. 328-29 (XXII. 292).
75. *Ibid.*, pp. 329-30 (XXII. 293).
76. *Ibid.*, pp. 330-31 (XXII. 294).
77. *Ibid.*, pp. 331-33 (XXII. 295-97).
78. *Ibid.*
79. *Ibid.*, pp. 333-34 (XXII. 298-99).
80. *Ibid.*, pp. 334-46 (XXII. 300-315).
81. Nyanaponika, *Buddhist Meditation*, pp. 23 and 34-46.

82. *The Dialogues of the Buddha* II (*Sacred Books*, III, 346 [Dīgha Nikāya XXII. 315]).
83. See ch. 1, "Personal Religion," pp. 50-53.
84. Nyanaponika, *Buddhist Meditation*, pp. 36-44.
85. *The Dialogues of the Buddha* I (*Sacred Books*, II, 26 ff. [Dīgha Nikāya I. 12 ff]).
86. *Gautama the Buddha*, p. 37.
87. As told in Edward Conze, *Buddhist Meditation* (Torchbooks; New York: Harper, 1969), pp. 79-80.

Chapter 4. From Imperative to Ethic

1. *Politics of Experience*, p. 25.
2. Quoted in *Varieties*, pp. 34-35.
3. *LSD*, p. 167.
4. See ch. 1, p. 22.
5. *Varieties*, pp. 216-19.
6. *LSD*, p. 160.
7. Novak says, "The drive which ultimately gives sense to all my diffuse actions is a unifying, meaning-giving drive. It is that drive which even in atheists and agnostics, I wish to call the religious drive: it ties one's life together" (*Ascent of the Mountain*, p. 3). I am using "impulse" in a way similar to Novak's "drives," although I am restricting the notion of "religious impulse" to include only those drives which claim a Sacred referent.
8. Social mores and customs are bound up with religious norms in a chicken-and-egg relationship. Therefore, chronological relationships are often hard to establish. Furthermore, distinctions between social and religious norms are not always clear, as when political and social documents (e.g., the U.S. Constitution) mingle religious concerns with social ones. It might be added that the process of socialization includes incorporation of religious practices into secular events and practices (e.g., prayer before athletic contests or civic gatherings). For a discussion of social adoption of religious ideas and practices, see: *American Civil Religion*, ed. Russel E. Richey and Donald G. Jones (New York: Harper, 1974).
9. See H. Richard Niebuhr, *Christ and Culture* (Torchbooks; New York: Harper, 1956).
10. "Introduction," *Patterns of Ethics in America Today*, ed. F. Ernest Johnson (New York: Harper, 1960), p. 3.
11. *Worship in Ancient Israel*, p. 38, n. 6.
12. *History of Israelite Religion*, pp. 84-85.
13. *Ibid.*, p. 85.
14. This cultic prohibition of idols was an uncommon, perhaps even a unique, characteristic of early Yahwist worship.
15. *Worship in Ancient Israel*, p. 39.
16. *Introduction to the Old Testament*, trans. David E. Green (Nashville: Abingdon Press, 1968), pp. 133-43.

17. Rowley, *Worship in Ancient Israel*, pp. 44 ff.
18. Fohrer, *History of Israelite Religion*, p. 82.
19. Compare Frederick Streng, *Understanding Religious Man* (Belmont, Cal.: Dickenson Publishing Company, 1969), p. 65.
20. *History of Israelite Religion*, p. 85.
21. Art Rosenblum, quoted by Ron E. Roberts in his *New Communes* (Englewood Cliffs, N.J.: Prentice Hall, 1971), p. 15.
22. The "first and great commandment" can be found in the famous Hebrew proclamation contained in Deut. 6:4-5. Likewise the "second commandment" is expressed in Lev. 19:18.
23. Millar Burrows, *An Outline of Biblical Theology* (Philadelphia: Westminster Press, 1946), p. 161.
24. *Ibid.*, p. 242.
25. *Ibid.*, p. 160.
26. Richard H. Hiers, *Jesus and Ethics: Four Interpretations* (Philadelphia: Westminster Press, 1968), p. 158.
27. This story is my retelling of the tale appearing in Henry Clarke Warren, *Buddhism in Translation* (New York: Atheneum, 1963), pp. 297-98 (*Visuddhi-Magga*, ch. 1).
28. *Ibid.*, pp. 298-300.
29. Drummond, *Gautama the Buddha*, p. 74.
30. See *Jataka Tales*, trans. H. T. Francis and E. J. Thomas (Bombay: Jaico Publishing House, 1956).
31. *Gautama the Buddha*, p. 107.
32. Detached intentionality is the foundation of the Four Noble Truths. Suffering in the world (First Truth) arises as a consequence of craving (Second Truth), and cessation of craving is possible (Third Truth) by nonattachment. The eightfold path is the formal guide to the proper nonattachment (Fourth Truth). Most scholars agree that the Four Aryan (Noble) Truths constitute the essential teachings of the Buddha himself. See: Drummond, *Gautama the Buddha*, p. 85; and T. W. and C. A. F. Rhys Davids, "Introduction," *The Dialogues of the Buddha* II (*Sacred Books*, III, 322). For a treatment of the Noble Truths, see: Rahula, *What the Buddha Taught*, pp. 16-66; Thomas, *Life of the Buddha*, pp. 81-96; and Chen, *Light of Asia*, pp. 30-46.
33. *The Dialogues of the Buddha* II (*Sacred Books*, III, 337-38 [Dīgha Nikāya II. 305]).
34. Chen's translation of terms in *Light of Asia*, p. 33 (Dīgha Nikāya II. 311).
35. *Ibid.*
36. *The Dialogues of the Buddha* II (*Sacred Books*, III, 343 [Dīgha Nikāya II. 311]).
37. *Ibid.*, p. 344 (II. 312). The two types of kindly concern for others may be generally divided into (1) "the desire of removing bane and sorrow (from one's fellow-men)," which is *karma*, and (2) "the desire of bringing (to one's fellow-men) that which is welfare and

NOTES TO PAGES 147-156

good," or *mettā*. Therefore, *karma* is, at times, called "preventive love," while *mettā* is "active love." See *The Pali Text Society's Pali-English Dictionary*, ed. T. W. Rhys Davids and William Stede (London: Luzac & Company, 1966), pp. 197 and 537 (under the terms "karmā" and "mudutā").

38. *Gautama the Buddha*, p. 88.
39. Pande, *Origins of Buddhism*, pp. 527-28. See *The Book of the Kindred Sayings* I (*Translation Series*, VII, 173-74 [Saṃyutta Nikāya I. 138]).
40. See *The Dialogues of the Buddha* I (*Sacred Books*, II, 300-320 [Dīgha Nikāya I. 235 ff.]); and Thomas, *Life of the Buddha*, pp. 125-27.
41. *What the Buddha Taught*, p. 46.
42. *The Dhammapada* (I. 1, 2, 5), trans. Irving Babbitt (New York: New Directions, 1965), p. 3.
43. Warren, *Buddhism in Translation*, p. 397.

Chapter 5. Religious Reflection and World Construction

1. *Ascent of the Mountain*, p. 177.
2. The various traditions of personal and social religion are transmitted orally prior to appearing in written form. A second step in the process of transmission is formal recognition (*i.e.*, canonization) of certain oral and/or written traditions, which are then considered "official" by a particular religious group or institution. Such finalizing steps were taken by the Jews at the Council at Jamnia in A.D. 90, by the early Christians in the late second century A.D. with the Muratorian canon, and by the Buddhists at the Council of Rājagṛaha immediately after the death of the Buddha (c. 480 B.C.). Since the final canon often is debated for centuries (e.g., Christian Council of Nicea in A.D. 325), the scriptural descriptions and proclamations that come down to a modern reader have often circuitously wound their way through many centuries, cultures, and minds, and only dimly reflect their originating impulses. Furthermore, the essentially different functions of reflective and expressive myths are hidden in the composite and complex literary process that presents varying mythic traditions as the product of one hand, one time, or one intention.
3. For a full discussion of religion as a product of social forces and human needs mediated by "symbols," see Clifford Geertz, "Religion as a Cultural System," *Anthropological Approaches to the Study of Religion*, ed. Michael Banton, A. S. A. Monographs 3 (London: Ravistock Publications, 1966), pp. 1-46. On the question of suffering as a religious problem, see pp. 19 ff.
4. Berger discusses death as a problem that religion "cosmicizes" in order to minimize. See *Sacred Canopy*, pp. 43-44.
5. *Varieties*, p. 75.

6. *Politics of Experience*, p. 17.
7. Berger and Luckmann discuss four different levels of legitimation from archaic to symbolic in *Social Construction*, pp. 92-95.
8. *Ibid.*, p. 155.
9. *Ibid.*, pp. 157-58.
10. *Ibid.*, p.157.
11. *Ibid.*, p.158.
12. See Berger, *Sacred Canopy*, pp. 88 ff.
13. It should be apparent that the analysis of Berger and Luckmann accounts for the realms of personal and social religion in their notions of objective and subjective aspects of socialization. What I find lacking in their analysis is a balance in the dialectic between man and society, personal experience and social formulation. What begins as a dialectic in their analysis becomes a skewed emphasis on social causality. Therefore, while I am using their concepts of plausibility structures and legitimations, I do not accept their implicit claim that the dialectic is actually not a dialectic at all but is a social dependency of exprience. It is when dealing with theology in social religion that my analysis most closely approximates theirs. The theology given birth in the institutionalization process would seem to be the set of religious assertions and formulations furthest removed from personal experience.
14. Berger, *Sacred Canopy*, p. 29.
15. *Ibid.*, pp. 31-32.
16. *Social Construction*, p. 110.
17. *Ibid.*, p.112.
18. *Ibid.*, p.108.
19. *Ibid.*, p.128.
20. See Novak, *Ascent of the Mountain*, p. 195. My explanation of sacred reality from the two perspectives of personal experience and social development can be viewed as a challenge to the social reality called "sociology of knowledge" and its legitimations. Still, my analysis is governed, to a great extent, by the language and society of which I find myself to be a part. The two basic assumptions I make, however, do not permit a sociologically relativistic outcome, but lead to the conclusion that my personal experiences have also determined the analysis I offer for consideration. Therefore, to some extent, it is a modified understanding of the nature of human experiences that separates my analysis from Berger and Luckmann's.
21. See "Ugaritic Myths and Epics: Poems about Baal and Anath," trans. H. L. Ginsberg in *The Ancient Near East: An Anthology of Texts and Pictures*, ed. James B. Pritchard (Princeton: Princeton University Press, 1958), pp. 92-118. For Akkadian myth, see "Akkadian Myths and Epics: The Creation Epic," trans. E. A. Speiser in *Ancient Near East*, pp. 32-39. See also Bernard W.

Anderson, *Creation versus Chaos* (New York: Association Press, 1967), pp. 15-22.

22. Harrelson, *Fertility Cult to Worship*, p. 2.
23. "Akkadian Myths and Epics," *Ancient Near East*, pp. 36-37.
24. *Israelite Religion*, p. 107.
25. A more synonymous use of creative speech with that in Genesis 1 can be found in an Old Egyptian myth (from Memphis, c. 1300 B.C.), which claims for Ptah, the god of Memphis, the creation of the whole world by an act of "heart and tongue." This Egyptian myth conceives the creation of all living things by the act of speech of Ptah (by his tongue) after he contemplates (in his heart) that to which he gives birth. The key to Ptah's creation is that "the tongue announces what the heart thinks." However, there is no mention in the Egyptian myth of a struggle with the primeval waters or of creation being an ordering process of such waters. Furthermore, the central place given to descriptions of Ptah and the frequent assertion of Ptah's lordship over all other gods lend credence to the supposition that the Memphitic creation myth was written as a justification of Ptah and his capital, Memphis, not as a description of how humankind came into being. See "Egyptian Myths and Tales: The Memphite Theology of Creation," trans. John A. Wilson, in *Ancient Near East*, pp. 1-2.
26. Gerhard von Rad, *Old Testament Theology*, trans D. M. G. Stalker, (New York: Harper, 1962), I, 136.
27. Ps. 8:3-8 is but one later indication of the Hebrews' recognition of their exalted—yet humble—status among all creatures.
28. *Old Testament Theology*, p. 136.
29. *Ibid.*, p. 141. Ringgren notes that the anti-serpent motif of the Jahwist story perhaps represents a polemic against the snake worship of the Canaanite Baal worshipers. However, the Jahwist description of Eden and its tree of life and rivers leads Ringgren to locate the origin of the story geographically in Mesopotamia in the Tigris and Euphrates river basin (*Israelite Religion*, p. 110). As we have already seen, the Priestly story parallels to some extent the Akkadian *Enūma elish*, and this would suggest that while differing in conception and expression, both the desert and sea myths likely shared common geographical territory. This does not mean that all persons who knew and accepted one myth would necessarily know or accept the other. What it does suggest is that speculation concerning the origin of the world and mankind in the ancient Near East was not limited to one motif or expression. Certainly it is not the case that the Hebrews were limited to one motif.
30. von Rad, *Old Testament Theology*, p. 136.
31. *Israelite Religion*, p. 105.
32. *Ibid.*, pp. 108-9.
33. As quoted in Anderson, *Creation versus Chaos*, p. 41.
34. *History of Israelite Religion*, p. 178.

35. *Old Testament Theology*, p. 138.
36. Rowley, *Worship in Ancient Israel*, p. 199.
37. *Creation versus Chaos*, p. 35.
38. *Israelite Religion*, p. 112. See also: Anderson, *Creation versus Chaos*, pp. 30-31; von Rad, *Old Testament Theology*, p. 139; and Fohrer, *History of Israelite Religion*, pp. 181-82.
39. Eliade, *Sacred and Profane*, p. 110.
40. *The Gospel According to John*, The Anchor Bible, Vol 29 (Garden City, N.Y.: Doubleday, 1966), p. 24.
41. John Marsh, *The Gospel of St. John*, The Pelican Gospel Commentaries, ed. D. E. Nineham (Baltimore: Penguin Books, 1968), p. 93. A consensus of scholarship points to the conclusion that the Prologue was a later addition to the Gospel of John, and that originally it did not include the material on John the Baptist (vss. 6-9 and 15) (Brown, *Gospel According to John*, pp. 3-4). Some commentators would exclude other verses (on the basis of literary and contextual criticism) from the original hymn composed in Johannine circles and added by the final redactor. For our use of this mythic hymn, however, it is important that the fully developed passage be considered, since it is the results of synthetic reflection we are examining.
42. See Brown, *Gospel According to John*, p. ciii; Bultmann, *Theology of the New Testament* II, 5-6; and C. H. Dodd, *The Interpretation of the Fourth Gospel* (Cambridge: The University Press, 1953), pp. 3-6.
43. For a rather complete discussion of the question of authorship, see Brown, *Gospel According to John*, pp. lxxxvii-xcviii.
44. Ibid., p. xxxiv-xxxvi, and Marsh, *St. John*, pp. 77-78.
45. Bultmann, *Primitive Christianity*, pp. 162-71 and 196-208. Bultmann modifies his assertion when he says that the primary source of John might have been the "gnosticizing Judaism" represented by the Essene community, in *Theology of the New Testament* II, 13.
46. Brown, *Gospel According to John*, p. lix. In various ways, all of the following cultural systems have been offered as supplying John with some aspect of his thought: Greek philosophy (especially Platonism and Stoicism), Gnosticism (especially the Mandaean and Hermetic traditions), Iranian or "Oriental" dualistic traditions, Hellenistic Judaism (e.g., Philo of Alexandria), apocalyptic forms of Judaism (e.g., Essenes), and earlier Christian traditions. See: *Ibid.*, pp. lii—lxvi; Marsh, *St. John*, pp. 31-39; Dodd, *Fourth Gospel*, pp. 10-130; and in a more general way, Albright, *From the Stone Age*, pp. 334-80.
47. Marsh, *St. John*, p. 96.
48. Brown, *Gospel According to John*, p. 14.
49. The added portions about John the Baptist (vss. 6-9, 15) seem to underscore what the hymn says about Jesus by stressing that John

was not the light and that Jesus was. Some scholars interpret these stanzas as anti-John polemic. For example, Brown, *Gospel According to John*, pp. 27-28.

50. Bultmann, *Theology of the New Testament* II, 13.
51. Brown, *Gospel According to John*, p. 26.
52. Marsh, *St. John*, p. 99.
53. Grant, *Roman Hellenism and the New Testament*, p. 118.
54. Dodd, *Fourth Gospel*, p. 296, and Marsh, *St. John*, p. 96.
55. Brown, *Gospel According to John*, p. lxix.
56. My retelling of "The Great Retirement," *Buddhism in Translations*, pp. 56-58 (Nidāna Katha I. 58-59).
57. From the Sutta Nipata, as quoted in Pande, *Buddhist Origins*, p. 374.
58. Chen, *Light of Asia*, p. 20.
59. Thomas, *Life of the Buddha*, p. 51.
60. Pande, *Origins of Buddhism*, p. 376.
61. *The Dialogues of the Buddha* II (*Sacred Books*, III, 167 [Dīgha Nikāya II. 151]).
62. *The Book of the Gradual Sayings* I (*Translation Series*, XXII, 119-21 [Anguttara Nikāya III. 4. 34.]).
63. Ibid., pp. 121-25 (III. 4. 35).
64. Ibid., pp. 128-29 (III. 4. 38; cf. Majjhima Nikāya I. 163).

BZ 78
.8516

Shinn, Larry D.

Two Sacred Worlds

DATE DUE
